SEND FORTH WITH HONOR

SEND FORTH WITH HONOR

HELPS FOR PARENTS OF MISSIONARIES

DR. RANDY L. BOTT

Millennial Press
Salt Lake City, Utah

Millennial Press, Inc.
11968 South Doves Landing Drive
Riverton, Utah 84065

Publisher's Cataloging-in-Publication Data
(Provided by Quality Books, Inc.)

Bott, Randy L., 1945–
  Send forth with honor: helps for parents of missionaries /
Randy L. Bott. — 1st ed.
    p. cm.
    Includes index.
    Preassigned LCCN: 97-74851
    ISBN 0-9660231-1-0
    1. Church of Jesus Christ of Latter-day Saints—Missions—
Handbooks, manuals, etc. 2. Mormon Church—Missions—Handbooks,
manuals, etc. 3. Mormon families—Handbooks, manuals, etc.
4. Missionaries—Family relationships. 5. Parent and teenager—
Religious aspects—Church of Jesus Christ of Latter-day Saints.
I. Title.

BX8661.B683 1997   266'.'9332
                                           QBI97-41298

To my wife, Vickie, and our six children, who exemplify the principles discussed in this work. To our children, who, although very normal children, at the time of this printing, two have served missions, two are currently serving, and two are preparing to serve. To the hundreds of missionaries who served with us in the California Fresno Mission and their families who allowed us to see into their hearts and homes on how they prepared, supported, and welcomed home their missionaries. To the countless Latter-day Saints who frequently ask how to more effectively participate in the great missionary work of the latter days, I dedicate this volume.

Contents

HELPING YOUR MISSIONARY PREPARE

1 Preparing Your Missionary to Serve with Honor. . . 2
2 The Decision to Serve. 6
3 Preparing Your Missionary to Enter the Temple . . 13
4 Pre-run on Missionarylike Activities. 24
5 Look and Act the Part 31
6 Overcoming Goliaths–Physical and Emotional . . . 40
7 Help Me Rise 50
8 Standing Alone If Necessary 59
9 Control from Within 68
10 Who Am I?. 76

**HELPING YOUR MISSIONARY SERVE
WITH HONOR**

11 Helping Your Missionary Deal
   with Homesickness. 90
12 Helping Your Missionary Be Obedient 99
13 Leadership and Your Missionary 111
14 Getting the Most I Possibly Can 118
15 Being Part of Your Missionary's Mission. 127
16 Serving Valiantly to the End 137

HELPING YOUR MISSIONARY RETURN
WITH HONOR

17 Understand Me. 148

18 Stand Independently Valiant 157

19 Using the Lessons 165

20 Continuing the Test. 174

21 When a Noble One Falters. 182

22 "Well Done Thou Good and Faithful Servant" . . 192

HELPING YOUR MISSIONARY PREPARE

1

PREPARING YOUR MISSIONARY TO SERVE WITH HONOR

MOST RIGHTEOUS LATTER-DAY SAINT PARENTS DREAM of the time when their children will be able to serve missions. Besides the personal growth the missionaries themselves experience, blessings both spiritual and financial come to the families of the missionaries. Eternal focus is fostered and cemented. Although the farewell, the Missionary Training Center experience, the airport, and the separation are difficult, the joy of welcoming home an honorably returning missionary far outweighs the price of separation.

Unfortunately, some missionaries do not have such a positive mission experience. The reasons could be many, but most are within our power to control. Lack of adequate preparation discourages some prospective missionaries from even applying. Staying worthy to serve becomes a monumental task in a world seemingly bent on spiritual suicide. The difficulty of the actual mission experience is greater than many expect. Those not properly warned and prepared for the totally new experiences of the mission field may find themselves overwhelmed, discouraged, and ready to "call it quits." Some face unusually challenging living conditions, companion problems, or health concerns. Others are unprepared for the onslaught of temptations and trials the adversary will throw in their way as they try to serve. Problems do not automatically cease when the missionary is released. Many returning missionaries report that the transition to "civilian life" is more difficult than the adjustment to the mission field. How we hurt for those young men and women who return home and lose their bearings. Isn't there something we can do to help them readjust without so much trauma?

Whatever the combination of circumstances, it is a sad day when a noble son or daughter comes home before the appointed release date defeated, downtrodden, and self-incriminating. Can those heartbreaks be avoided? In most instances the answer is a resounding "Yes!" But it will take a sustained effort on the part of the missionary, the parents, other members of the immediate and extended families and, hopefully, the missionary's friends.

How to be supportive may not be as evident as we have assumed. Although ideas may vary, certain principles can direct our efforts and help us avoid being counterproductive to the goal of preparing, sending and sustaining, and welcoming home honorable missionaries.

In an attempt to influence directly the young man or woman who is preparing for a mission, I have written a book entitled *"Prepare with Honor."* Having participated in and observed firsthand the struggles of full-time missionaries, I wrote a second book entitled *"Serve with Honor."* I discussed many challenges posing the greatest problems to the missionaries, including practical suggestions about how to cope with such situations encountered in the mission field. After listening to returned missionaries complain about the difficulty of staying active and spiritually motivated upon their return, and witnessing the number who waver in their commitment to sustained spirituality, I wrote a third book entitled *"Home with Honor."*

With the idea in mind of providing parents with some suggestions to interface with their children more effectively in all three phases of missionary work (preparing, serving, and returning), I am writing this final volume. You may have some definite ideas about other effective ways of handling some of the challenges discussed in this volume. By all means, use those ideas to strengthen your sons and daughters. In the event you do not have a well-thought- out plan or possibly have not considered the issues discussed, this book may act as a catalyst to aid you in helping your children.

Many of the ideas discussed in this book parallel those found in the three previously mentioned books. More will be said in this book about your support role that is not mentioned at all in those other books. You do not need to purchase those volumes in order to understand what is written in this book. The intention is to make this book stand on its own content. However, you may find the information discussed in the other books very beneficial to your son or daughter.

Rearing children in the "last days" is challenging at best. Even the most diligent parents may face heartbreaking situations which may cause us to question our methods and effectiveness. Whether a young man or young woman chooses to serve a mission is a personal decision. You cannot, nor should you want to, force someone to go. Too many challenges in the mission field require personal commitment. When the going in the mission field gets tough (and it will!) the missionary needs to realize he or she (not you) made the decision to serve.

Many of the items discussed in this book will help you understand the proper procedure for handling emergencies, questions, making calls and contacts, or just getting answers on what to expect. Even after having served as a mission president, I felt frustrated at times in coping with the problems our two daughters were facing as missionaries in far-off France and Spain. Many practical tips are the result of my contacting the Missionary Committee of The Church of Jesus Christ of Latter-day Saints for clarifications.

Because we belong to a dynamic church, policies concerning missionaries may change. However, the principles behind the policies will remain constant. You should be rightfully proud to be entrusted by our Heavenly Father with the awe-inspiring task of preparing the missionary force who will take the gospel into the most remote parts of the globe in preparation for the great second coming of the Lord. Are you up to the challenge? Ready or not, the challenge is real and the time is now. Using the gospel as the standard, you will not disappoint the Lord as you prepare your sons and daughters to *Serve with Honor.*

2

....

THE DECISION TO SERVE

When is the best time to start talking about a mission? It would probably be all right to wait until you are out of the delivery room! Some parents seem to take the "wait-and-see" approach. "We'll let the child choose for himself or herself," they say. It sounds like such a nice, democratic way, but it is in direct opposition to the counsel of the Lord and his leaders. The Lord spoke plainly in the early days of the Church concerning his expectations of missionary service by young men. He said: "And now this calling and commandment give I unto you concerning all men. . . . And this commandment shall be given unto the elders of my church, that *every man* which will embrace it [the gospel] with singleness of heart may be ordained and *sent forth*, even as I have spoken" (D&C 36:4, 7; emphasis added).

President Spencer W. Kimball gave the following thought-provoking advice:

A mission is not just a casual thing . . . it is not an alternative program in the Church. Neither is a mission a matter of choice any more than tithing is a choice, any more than sacrament meeting is a choice, any more than the Word of Wisdom is a choice. Of course, we have our free agency, but the Lord has given us choices. We can do as we please. We can go on a mission or we can remain home. But every normal young man is as much obligated to go on a mission as he is to pay his tithing, attend his meetings, keep the Sabbath day holy, and keep his life spotless and clean. (Address to Seminary and Institute Personnel, BYU, June 28, 1968)

President Kimball also stated: "Every boy in every country in all the world who has been baptized and received the Holy Ghost will have the responsibility of bearing the message of the gospel to the people of the world. And this is also your opportunity, and it will contribute greatly towards your greatness" (Conference Report, Oct. 1974, p. 117).

President Kimball's counsel was reconfirmed by President Ezra Taft Benson when he said: "Not only should a mission be regarded as a priesthood duty, but every young man should look forward to this experience with great joy and anticipation. What a sacred privilege to serve the Lord full time for two years with all your heart, might, mind and strength.

"You can do nothing more important. School can wait. Scholarships can be deferred. Occupational goals can be postponed. Yes, even temple marriage should wait until after a young man has served an honorable mission for the Lord" (*Church News*, May 18, 1986, p. 3).

The counsel for young women to serve missions is somewhat different. In the April 1988 general conference, President Ezra Taft Benson said: "As a single sister, where marriage is not in your immediate future, have you prayed about serving a full-time mission and sought counsel from your parents and your bishop? Our single sisters are serving marvelous missions throughout the world" (*Ensign*, May 1988, p. 84).

In a special meeting for premissionaries at Brigham Young University on November 16, 1994, Elder Richard G. Scott said young women should not feel pressured to go on missions. Although they constitute some of the most powerful missionaries in the world, marriage should take precedence over missions when the opportunity presents itself.

Counsel like that does not leave much question in the mind of the true Saint. It is not difficult to emphasize "when" rather than "if" as we talk about the future with our children. "*When* you are on your mission you will need to know . . ." "You will make such a great teacher *when* you are on your mission." "Would you like to learn a language in school so you will be prepared *when* you are called to serve?" (emphasis added). The opportunities are endless. We have found, as parents, our boys quickly adopted the same "when" reference as they talk about the future. There just is not any question college will be postponed, marriage will be deferred, jobs will be put on hold, and spending for "toys" (trucks, motorcycles, boats, etc.) will be modified so they do not interfere with missions.

Many times as a mission president I would ask the newly arrived missionaries in the entrance interview how long they had been preparing for their missions. There was a noticeable difference between those who had been preparing all their lives and those who decided only a few months earlier. Although many of the missionaries came from troubled homes, there was still real power with those who, with obvious pride, said how much Mom and Dad were behind them in serving. It was difficult for those who came without parental support. Many served honorably but with added burdens when the parents would flood them with a barrage of letters condemning their service as a "waste of time" or constantly encouraging them to abandon their mission and come home.

If you are fortunate enough to have missionaries serving in your ward or branch, point them out as role models for your children. Some missionaries who are still struggling also provide some very positive teaching moments for your children. Although we should not publicly (or privately) criticize the missionaries who are now serving, there is real value in discussing with our children areas of needed improvement and mistakes that could be avoided.

Missionary farewells and welcome home meetings are highly motivational for our youth. The difference between those who are going and those who are returning is obvious to everyone. It is not just the eighteen months or two years in age difference. It is light years in spiritual maturity. Commenting on the polish and poise of a returning missionary is a form of positive reinforcement to your son or daughter who usually would very much like to please you. If you happen to be unfortunate enough to observe a "returned missionary" who has been away from home for only a couple of years, he or she also provides a unique opportunity to teach your children that serving an honorable mission requires more than just being away from home.

Writing letters to missionaries on their birthdays, Christmas, or other times has dual positive results. Missionaries love to receive letters, and the letters you receive in return will enthuse your children more than almost anything else. If the missionaries fail to write back, this too can be a powerful teaching moment. Mention to your children how disappointed you are that Elder So-and-So did not acknowledge your letter. It is a wonderful time to let them know how much you are looking forward to their weekly letters when they go.

Prayers morning, mealtime, and night all provide excellent opportunities for you to express, in the presence of your children, your concern and love for those who are serving. It is beneficial to pray occasionally for your sons and daughters who are preparing to serve. It is also illuminating to note how often in our public prayers in sacrament meeting and other church meetings the person acting as voice prays for "the missionaries." Bedtime stories from the Scriptures and the accounts of missionaries in the early days of the Church can be combined with stories about when you may have served or about missionaries you know who have served. This is a missionary church. General conference talks are often geared towards encouraging young men and women to prepare. Many *Ensign, New Era,* and *Friend* articles deal with missionary work. Family home evening lessons and demonstrations can focus on different aspects of missionary life. Wall hangings, thoughts on the refrigerator, notes in sack lunches, mission- related music and songs all contribute to offset the satanic pull away from missionary service.

It is a fact that most of the young men who are deacon age (12–13) say they are planning on a mission. Somewhat fewer make the same commitment when they are teacher age (14–15). The downward trend continues when the young men reach priest age (16–18) but the percentage of those who are still planning on serving a mission is still very high. Between their eighteenth and nineteenth birthdays, the percentage plummets to about 25 percent worldwide and approximately 33 percent in the United States and Canada. What happens? It is easy to say you are going until the time comes to fill out the papers and start the physical preparation process. Then reality hits! Instead of just talk, there needs to be action. Those whose commitment has been superficial—just to get the parents, priesthood leaders, and others off their backs—find ways of going back on their commitment to serve. If the commitment has been constant and lifelong, when the time for the paperwork comes the excitement only heightens. If a young person really wants to serve, he or she will find a way; if not, he or she will find an excuse.

Is a mission a scary thing? Yes, to most young men and women it is. It is something we look forward to, yet it is an uncharted trail. We have never been along that path before and must exercise tremendous faith in ourselves and the Lord to take that quantum step. If we, as parents and support people, have done our job, the decision is much easier to make. Knowing everyone is behind them and there to make sure they do not fail will shore up the sagging confidence.

We could greatly increase our children's understanding of the privilege it is to serve if we would help them put it in proper perspective. Currently, approximately 50,000 missionaries are serving worldwide. With a world population which exceeds five billion, that means that there are more than 100,000 people for every Latter-day Saint missionary! Is it any wonder that Satan focuses his attention on trying to dissuade or disqualify as many as possible from serving?

We must teach our children that they aren't just another nameless face in the sea of humanity. They have been chosen and reserved from before the foundation of the world to serve now. Satanic opposition is a given. How we teach them to cope with the opposition makes all the difference in the world.

3

....

PREPARING YOUR MISSIONARY TO ENTER THE TEMPLE

IN THE PRESS OF TRYING TO KEEP UP with our children as they enter the teen years, it is easy to overlook the most important of all preparations—going to the temple. From the time children are very little, pictures of temples should be placed in their rooms. They should be permitted to watch you and your husband or wife prepare for regular temple excursions. You should talk frequently about the Spirit you feel when you attend the temple. If the occasion arises, take them to a temple open house prior to its dedication or rededication.

In addition to the many things you can talk about (which we will discuss later in the chapter), remember to take advantage of the sacredness of the temple site itself. Those grounds were consecrated to the Lord at the time of the temple dedication. Walking around the temple grounds as a family may not seem that significant to you, but to young people who have never been within the walls, the Spirit may be more noticeable than it is to you. Special family picnics with a family home evening lesson about temples prior to visiting the visitor's center or just walking the grounds may have a powerful impact. After touring the grounds or the visitor's center, make a point of going out for a treat or back to a park for dessert. Ending with dessert can leave a sweet taste in your children's mouths and sweet memories in the recesses of their minds.

Those parents who have regularly attended the temple may recognize that the adversary seems to double his efforts to prevent the temple experience from being a totally positive one. If we are prepared for what might occur, we can increase our defenses. It is likely that one or more of our children will have a bad day or will be uncooperative. It is just as likely that the car will have problems or run out of gas. If you are prepared, those potentially explosive situations become humorous. Warn the kids well in advance of the likelihood of such opposition. Then when it happens, identify it with them and work together to overcome the obstacle.

At family home evenings we can sing songs about the temple. The Primary songs are addictive (in a good way) and really drive home the point. At planned intervals during the year, focus on preparing to go to the temple. As your sons receive the Aaronic Priesthood emphasize that now they can go to the temple to do baptisms for the dead. Take your sons and daughters to the temple (if one is located within a reasonable distance from home) and do baptisms for the dead. We have found it to be a very unifying experience for the family.

As you drive to and return home from the temple, turn off the radio and talk about why we do ordinance work for the dead. One of the exercises I do with my Sharing the Gospel classes at BYU is to have all the ones who have not yet been through the temple raise their hands. That is usually 90 percent of the class. Then I ask them to answer the question posed by an inquisitive nonmember: "What do you Mormons do in your secretive temples?" Since most of them have never been there, I usually draw a classroom full of blank looks. I then disengage and tell them we'll approach the answer to that question from a different direction.

I then ask them to list for me the ordinances a person must perform before they can go to the highest degree of the celestial kingdom. With a little prompting they identify five ordinances: (1) Baptism, (2) Reception of the Holy Ghost, (3) Priesthood for the men, (4) Endowment, and (5) Sealing to a mate. Then I ask the question again: "What do you Mormons do in your secretive temples?" It is like a light turning on in their minds. A hand goes up and excitedly a young person will say, "Why we do the same five ordinances for the dead that are required of those that are living. We literally become saviors on Mt. Zion in doing for them what they did not have the opportunity to do for themselves while on the earth." That is exactly correct.

The answer is so simple when we stand back and see the justice of God in giving every one of his sons or daughters the opportunity to accept the ordinances of salvation and exaltation. Whether they receive them personally here on the earth themselves or have the ordinance work done for them by living proxies and then have the ordinances validated when they receive the gospel in the spirit world, it makes no difference. As you work with your children, they begin to see that doing missionary work isn't separate and apart from doing temple work. They begin to see the mission of the Church not as three separate and distinct missions (that is, proclaiming the gospel, redeeming the dead, and perfecting the Saints), but as three integrated parts of a single mission—to prepare the sons and daughters of God to return to his presence and live with him eternally.

If our experience in teaching our children is typical, it will require more than a single session to permanently embed the concept in their minds. Frequent teaching and reteaching, allowing them to participate to the degree they are able (for example, doing baptisms for the dead), and frequent experiences at the temple grounds will keep their young minds focused on the temple.

When emphasis for preparing for the future includes going to the temple, it is much easier to help our children avoid the problems which are so prevalent in their world. Sometimes going to the celestial kingdom is so distant in their young minds that it isn't real. However, the visual presence of the temple with the prospect of going there in the near future is much more likely to act as a motivator to help them avoid the polluting effects of the world. Reminding children that breaking the Word of Wisdom keeps people from entering the temple helps strengthen their resolve to avoid those harmful substances. When you lament over a young person who had to postpone his endowment date because of moral problems or a young couple who had to be married civilly and then wait for a year before going to the temple, the chances increase that your children will think twice before forfeiting their right to enter the temple.

The temple is a visual reminder that God expects his children to live apart from the world. If the temple hasn't made a noticeable difference in the way you treat each other as husband and wife, or the way you treat your children, or the way you conduct your business affairs, or the way you serve in your church calling, then why wonder if your children set no premium on preparing for the temple themselves? The key to helping our children develop a burning desire to attend the temple is the observable difference the temple makes in our own lives. With very little effort we can reinforce in their young minds the difference the temple makes in us. Little statements like "I gave the extra change back to the cashier at the grocery store because I promised in the temple that I would be totally honest," or "I don't get as upset at others because I learned in the temple to have more godly patience," or "I don't mind the hours I spend serving in the Church because I promised in the temple I would do whatever the Lord wants me to do"—these kinds of statements make a huge difference in the minds of our children as the Spirit reminds them of where we learned the principles of godliness (see D&C 84:19-22).

Ironically many of our young people have serious misperceptions about what goes on in the temple. This seems to be especially true of young women. Although there are many things we should not discuss with them before they go to the temple, there are many that we should. They should be reassured that their modesty will not be compromised in the least in the temple. You need only to get the youth talking about what they expect the temple to be like and you'll rapidly discover the need to be more open in discussing what really goes on there. One young woman all but called me a liar because I assured her that she would not be expected to parade naked before the ordinance workers. She had been "psyching" herself to do whatever was required to receive her endowment and she did not want me to give her a false assurance. One quick phone call to the temple president restored her image of me as an honest bishop.

One of the factors which can be addressed to lessen

the surprise of the first-time templegoer is to have parents, priesthood leaders, or designated teachers address the idea of learning by symbolic presentation rather than by strictly realistic presentation. Too many young people report that they were surprised at the rituals and symbolism found in the temple. One of the most beautiful parts of the entire endowment session is to look behind the symbol and see the Lord teaching us how to successfully cope with the adversary and our present world. If people (young or old) do not learn to see beyond the symbol, they will miss 99 percent of what the temple ceremonies are all about.

Although it would be inappropriate to try to teach people what the symbols mean (the Lord will do that by the power of the Spirit as the individual is prepared), it is not out of line to help them understand the concept of symbolic teaching. For example, the sacramental use of bread and water represents the body and blood of the Savior. Baptism is symbolic of burying the "old man of sin" (see Romans 6:3-6) and being reborn as a new, clean person. To most Christians the cross is a symbol of the death of Christ. In the Old Testament the entire law of Moses was symbolic of the future sacrifice of the Son of God (see Alma 34:14). Red lights don't really mean "Stop" at an intersection. They are symbols that helps us interpret the intention of the semaphore signal no matter what language we speak. You may want to discuss symbolism and go into much more depth than I have touched upon here in helping prepare your children for their initial temple experience. The one thing I would emphasize is that they will not completely understand the deep, beautiful meaning of the temple on their first time through. No one does. In fact it may take many years before the true meaning of the endowment begins to be revealed to them.

President Ezra Taft Benson reinforced the necessity of returning often to the temple to learn the full meaning of the endowment:

> I make it a practice, whenever I perform a marriage, to suggest to the young couple that they return to the temple as soon as they can and go through the temple again as husband and wife. It isn't possible for them to understand fully the meaning of the holy endowment or the sealing with one trip through the temple, but as they repeat their visits to the temple, the beauty, the significance, and the importance of it all will be emphasized upon them. I have later had letters from some of these young couples expressing appreciation because that item was emphasized particularly. As they repeat their visits to the temple, their love for each other tends to increase and their marriage tends to be strengthened. (*Teachings of Ezra Taft Benson* [Salt Lake City: Bookcraft, 1988], p. 258)

It is somewhat of a surprise to me to ask my very bright, young BYU students why they go to the temple. Many have not been instructed sufficiently to have more than a grade school understanding. I ask a follow-up question: "Why does the Church have you go to the temple before going on a mission?" Again far too many seem to be at a loss to explain. Occasionally a young man or woman will respond, "We go there to get our endowment before we go to serve." "What is the endowment you get?" I ask. Without going into too much detail, which again might be inappropriate, I explain that it is an endowment of knowledge and power—knowledge that will help them both in this life and in the life to come and power sufficient to accomplish their mortal mission and to return to the Father and gain eternal life. I also emphasize that the Lord gives us an endowment of knowledge and power to enable us to detect Satan in all his subtle forms and sufficient power to cast him out.

If our sons and daughters realize that the adversary will focus his evil attention on them in the mission field, it seems reasonable that the Lord will give them extra power to ward off the additional temptations. We can and should emphasize that we must live righteously to enjoy the additional protection. The Lord asks a question and gives an answer in the Doctrine and Covenants concerning the receiving of a gift:

> For what doth it profit a man if a gift is bestowed upon him, and he receive not the gift? Behold, he rejoices not in that which is given unto him, neither rejoices in him who is the giver of the gift. (D&C 88:33)

Too many missionaries and endowed members of the Church act as though the endowment is just another ritual in the Church. Without some deeper understanding of what it means and how it applies to them, they are apt to be overcome by the increased temptations of the adversary which are permitted with their reception of additional light and knowledge.

Usually there is a "Temple Preparation Seminar" taught on either the ward or stake level. Be sure to have your sons and daughters take the course before going to the temple. Also, some great books by General Authorities will help you prepare your sons and daughters. The main thing is "don't neglect this vital area of preparation."

Temple attendance involves covenant-making. Unless we have taken the time and paid the price to teach our children about making covenants with Heavenly Father, they may assume that it is just like making a contract with someone here on the earth. But there is a world of difference. Starting with the covenant they make at baptism, teach your children the difference between the way they have promised Heavenly Father that they would act and the way the world lives. There should be a multitude of examples you can use to illustrate how a covenant member of the Church is different from a nonmember. Word of Wisdom, chastity, tithing, church attendance, honesty, devotion to family—the list is almost endless.

As you continue teaching your children about making additional covenants, insure that they understand that we can't just break our covenant with Heavenly Father like we might break a promise to a friend, without incurring the just punishments from God. However, if we emphasize only the negative aspects of covenant-breaking, a young person might question the value of entering into the covenant in the first place. Therefore, we must make sure that we identify and explain the additional blessings which come from making the covenant. For example, with the additional expectations we take on ourselves at the time of baptism, we are also promised the right to the gift of the Holy Ghost. What good is the Holy Ghost? It almost sounds blasphemous to ask. But in order to illustrate the point, let's ask and answer the question. Joseph Smith explained one huge advantage of having the Spirit. "No man can receive the Holy Ghost without receiving revelations. The Holy Ghost is a revelator" (Joseph Fielding Smith, comp.,

Teachings of the Prophet Joseph Smith [Salt Lake City: Deseret Book, 1967], Section Six, 1843-44, p. 328).

The right to receive revelation from God to cope with the trials and challenges of life is no small matter. It is worth the sacrifice of the "fun" things of the world—which are really not beneficial at all. If you search the Scriptures and the teachings of the latter-day prophets, you will begin to compile a list of amazing blessings associated with the Holy Ghost. The sacrifices necessary to the companionship of the Holy Ghost seems unimportant compared to the blessings we receive. Using the "two ends of the stick" concept, you can illustrate the cause/effect relationship of covenants to blessings. If you pick up the end of the stick labeled "The Gift of the Holy Ghost," the other end of the stick contains numerous and wonderful blessings.

The same is true of the priesthood for the young men. When they covenant to receive the priesthood, more sacrifice and more commitment are required of them. Sometimes the requirements seem so overwhelming that they may wonder if getting the priesthood is worth it. They may wonder, that is, until they read and understand the Oath and Covenant of the Priesthood found in Doctrine and Covenants 84:33-40. Blessings like "all that the Father hath" go beyond human comprehension. Reading earlier in that same section (D&C 84:19-20), one can see that revelations necessary to understand the mysteries of God and God himself are associated with the ordinances of the priesthood.

What blessings are associated with the additional requirements of making the covenants found in the endowment received at the temple? Those blessings enable the faithful templegoer to come into the presence of the Lord (see D&C 84:21–22). There are so many blessings which enable the true temple attender to know how to be a more perfect husband or wife, father or mother, Church member. How to detect Satan and overcome his influence is a major blessing received by those who make covenants in the temple. A host of other blessings are available only to those who make and keep the covenants they made in the temple.

Just "going through the temple" will have little or no beneficial influence on individuals if they do not allow the temple to "go through them." The alarming increase in divorce between husbands and wives who have been married in the temple provides irrefutable evidence that there is room for improvement in how we teach our people to make and keep covenants. Somehow we must instill in our children that the temple provides the rock-solid foundation upon which we build our lives and our marriages. Casualness in our approach to keeping the covenants will never bring the promised blessings. We need to serve with all our heart, might, mind, and strength (see D&C 4:2) in order to stand blameless before God at the last day.

Although the task is serious and has potentially devastating results if we fail, we need not look with fear and trepidation at preparing our children for the temple. It is a joy to watch them respond to the promptings of the Spirit as they shed their teenage mantle and turn their focus toward the House of the Lord. A spurt now and then in temple preparation is far less desirable than a constant trickle over a number of years. Start preparing your children to enter the temple; their spiritual maturation will make your family life more pleasant now and more focused on spiritual things as the years pass.

4
....

PRE-RUN ON MISSIONARYLIKE ACTIVITIES

ANYTIME WE EMBARK ON A VENTURE that carries us into areas we have never been or into activities we have never participated in or demands we have yet to meet, we tend to get nervous.

The adversary is always there causing us to question our ability to successfully do what we have been called to do. This is especially true with missionaries. They pose too great a threat to Satan and his kingdom to ignore. If, as parents, we can identify what a missionary does, we can help our children experience before they submit their papers as many as possible of the experiences they will be having in the mission field. This chapter is to help identify areas of concern and give suggestions about how to help our children gain experience in those areas.

When we think of missionaries we think of two young men or young women teaching a family about the gospel. Immediately we can identify two possible anxiety-producing activities: (1) Teaching and (2) Teaching the gospel.

If you consider how often the Lord provides opportunities to teach, you will note that with a little conscious effort we can help young people overcome the fear of teaching. Let's list those opportunities. At least annually during their Aaronic Priesthood and Young Women's years, young men and women are supposed to be given an opportunity to talk in sacrament meeting. Unfortunately, too many young people either try to avoid the experience or defer to reading a story or article from the *New Era* for their talk.

As parents we need to take a more active role in helping them learn to prepare and present their talks. A talk read from a Church magazine does little to teach them either technique or confidence, although it may enhance their reading ability. How do you teach them to give a talk? It isn't difficult: First, help them decide on the "purpose" or "problem" on which they want to focus their talk. Ask them to answer the question "What do you want to accomplish in this talk?" They might have a purpose like "The purpose of my talk is to encourage members of the Church to read their scriptures on a daily basis." Or they might state the purpose in the form of a problem: "The problem with many members of the Church is they do not read scriptures together as a family on a regular basis." Once they have decided on a purpose or a problem, it will guide them in their preparation.

Next, with their purpose statement in front of you, ask them: "If you could say only two or three things about this topic, what would you say?" They may have trouble identifying what they want to talk about. Let them read a few articles or talks by General Authorities and see if they can identify the main point the person is trying to make. Make sure they limit themselves to two or three but never more than four major concepts. These are called "main ideas." They are so important that if the speaker before them takes almost all the time, they need at least enough time to read their main ideas before bearing their testimony and sitting down.

After they identify the main ideas, have them look for stories, illustrations, scriptures, and examples to enlarge upon each of the main ideas. Make sure each story helps clarify the main idea and is not just something to take up time. This section could be called "enlargements" because the items in this section do not stand alone but merely enlarge upon the main ideas. In the event the speaker before them takes too much time, they can cut their talks shorter by eliminating or shortening the examples, scriptures, etc. Never eliminate the main ideas! If a speaker does not show up and they have twice the assigned time to speak, no problem—they can just add some enlargement materials. They should not try to come up with a new *main idea*. So the buffer enabling them to lengthen or shorten their talk without sacrificing the main ideas is the enlargement section.

The final part of the talk is their testimony. Their testimony tells people how strongly they believe in what they have been saying. Make sure they do not wander all over with their testimony. Have them focus on the subject they have been talking about. When they set up their talk, they may want to use this format to keep on track:

Topic	
Purpose or Problem	Testimony
Main Ideas	Enlargements
1.	1. Illustrations
	A. Examples
	B. Stories
2.	C. Personal experiences
3.	2. Scriptures

Using the preceding method, they will find it very easy to stop exactly when they are assigned without sacrificing the central message of their talks. Those who have used this method find it easy and effective. If you have another method that really works, help them use it. Be careful not to assume that they already know how to prepare and deliver a talk just because they can carry on a conversation with you at home.

Once we help them get away from reading their talks, they will find public speaking is not as frightening as they thought. If the bishop is not following through on giving the youth opportunities to speak, you might suggest to him how important public speaking is in a young person's preparation.

Another teaching opportunity that comes as close to missionary work as is possible is home teaching and visiting teaching. Again, too many young people try to avoid going because "it isn't interesting." Let them assume some responsibility for the teaching. Avoid letting them read the "First Presidency Message" from the *Ensign*; have them tell it in their own words. Think about the parallels: two people sitting in a home other than their own, teaching the gospel of Jesus Christ. At least every month, experience should be gained that reduces, if not eliminates, the fear of teaching.

Family home evening provides a weekly experience when the gospel can be discussed in a nonthreatening environment. Gently encourage your children to prepare the lessons using the *Family Resource Book*, an old family home evening manual, or a priesthood or Relief Society manual. Make sure you give them opportunities to ask and answer questions. Get them in the habit of using examples, answering questions, and reading verbatim from the Scriptures. Until they become familiar with the cadence of the Scriptures, they will naturally have a built-in fear of reading them in public.

Isolated teaching experiences (preparation of a younger brother or sister for baptism, teaching about the priesthood to a younger brother, counseling the family about the death or illness of a grandparent) can all afford opportunities to project your prospective missionary into real-life situations. If they resist, you can explain your purpose for giving them the experience. Drawing an analogy between participating in a sport without training and the painful consequences that inevitably follow with going on a mission unprepared may help clarify in their minds the necessity of taking advantage of these opportunities.

With a little more creativity they will also be able to see that volunteering as a substitute teacher in Primary or Sunday School may not be a bad idea. Firesides and youth conferences, bishop youth firesides, and round table discussions also are available to those who really get enthused about teaching. Emphasize how vocal the youth are about hearing "boring talks" and challenge them to make their talks more interesting.

The second area that causes concern for young people is their panicked realization that they really do not know the gospel as well as they thought. They really are a smart group, but they seem to lose confidence as their missions approach. Some family-centered activities might help restore and increase their confidence. Challenge them to find answers from the Scriptures to gospel questions you pose. Games at family home evening in which questions are raised and answers given can be reassuring. Let them ask questions. That may be a little scary to you if you are not accustomed to being questioned on a level the depth of which may cause you some amazement. Although "Gospel Trivia" games are fun, try to focus on those questions young missionaries will likely meet in the mission field. There are available for computers gospel data bases which help prospective missionaries learn to find answers to difficult questions. Older brothers or sisters who have served a mission and other former missionaries may be a resource on questions that are currently being asked to missionaries.

As you discuss the gospel as a family, get in the habit of documenting your answers from the Scriptures. At first it may seem a little awkward, but as proficiency increases you will find it challenging and rewarding. Although it may pose a strain on the family food budget, it is extremely helpful to invite the full-time missionaries to dinner and have them describe what they are going through and what they wished they had done to prepare better. There just isn't anything as motivating as someone approximately your child's age who is doing exactly what he or she will be doing in the near future.

In order to increase their attentiveness in sacrament meeting, we encourage our children to try documenting the doctrine taught by the speakers. If they feel the doctrine is not accurate, they must find a scripture proving their point. Although they have a long way to go before proficiency is reached, it is helpful for their future missions and beneficial for the reverence of the meeting.

Family reading of the Scriptures really helps keep them going. The Book of Mormon is a must to read before they go, and more than passing familiarity with the other Scriptures is a huge plus for them. Basic books like *A Marvelous Work and Wonder* and the three volumes of *Doctrines of Salvation* teach the gospel in understandable language. *Truth Restored* gives a good basic background in Church history. More rapt attention in Seminary and Institute helps eat away at the ignorance base. Sometimes a favorite uncle, aunt, or older cousin can be the catalyst to get them motivated in their gospel study. Even if you are not totally successful in getting them immersed in gospel study, whatever you do is better than if they wait until they arrive at the MTC to begin their serious study.

One word of caution—although many writers are easier to read than the Scriptures, one must be particularly cautious about accepting everything in print as "the gospel truth." Encourage your premissionaries to search the words of the Apostles and prophets for doctrinal insights and answers before turning to secondary sources. If you are successful in igniting their curiosity about the gospel, you will be rewarded an hundred fold by the Spirit those discussions bring into your home. You will likely be amazed at the depth of the questions they will ask and the conversations they will want to engage in. It is not a crime to humbly admit "I don't know the answer to your question." If you are willing to reach out to those who do know, it will set an excellent example for your preparing missionary to follow both as a missionary and a maturing Latter-day Saint.

5

Look and Act the Part

IT WAS ALWAYS A DISAPPOINTMENT to see a young missionary arrive in the field who had not learned to take charge
of his or her own life. It was most noticeable during the
summer months when they would arrive after a three week
stay in the MTC. Many had received their "missionary
haircut" the Saturday night before their Sunday farewell.
The telltale lines between their suntan and their newly
adopted haircut line left little question that the standard
missionary haircut was not the norm. You might well be
asking yourself if I really believe parents can prevail on
their children to adopt a missionary hairstyle before
their mission. That is not what I'm about to suggest.

Joseph Smith taught a powerful lesson in his reply
when asked how he governed his people: "I teach them
correct principles and they govern themselves" (*Millennial Star* 13:339). During a Mission President's Seminar
in San Francisco in 1992, Elder Jacob de Jager (former
member of the First Quorum of Seventy and then a
member of our Area Presidency) said half jokingly, half
serious: "What Joseph really meant to say was 'I teach
and teach and teach and teach them correct principles
and hope they will govern themselves!" Amidst the
humor most parents can see the serious reality.

31

Perhaps I can preface my point with a personal example. During a zone conference early in our mission experience, we noticed the grooming and dress standards were starting to sag. When I mentioned the need to "look the part," I could hear a little murmuring coming from missionaries sitting on the back row. They thought the new president was a little fanatical and was asking too much. I decided to wait a month to teach the lesson.

At the beginning of the next zone conference, I announced that I was somewhat self-conscious since my hair is grey and thinning. I singled out an elder with a beautiful full head of hair and said I wished I could look like him. Then from my paper bag under the lectern I pulled a blond wig my children used as a dress-up. It looked like an "Annie wig" with corkscrew curls all over it. I put it on. The response was an immediate roar of laughter with the expected rolling of the eyeball, which silently meant "What kind of a strange duck did we get for a president?" Without responding to their outburst, I noted that my eyesight was beginning to fail but that I didn't want just the normal wire-rimmed glasses. I wanted something that made me stand out a little. From the same paper bag I pulled out a pair of Halloween glasses which measure about eighteen inches across. They were red, and when I put them on the response of the missionaries was what you would expect—near pandemonium. After they settled down a little I made a final statement. "I want you missionaries to know that an older guy can still be 'with it,' so I have carefully observed the 'in group' in California." With that introduction (not having to vie for their attention at all!), I took from my pocket one of my wife's gold-colored earrings (the clip-on type) and put it on one lobe of my nose. Without waiting for the comments to subside I said: "Now, if I could have your attention we will discuss the atonement of Christ for the next two hours." I opened my Scriptures and started the lesson. As you might expect, they were not quite ready to settle down. I urged them to get serious and start our study session. Finally, from the back row, one elder spoke up: "President, please take that stuff off. We can't concentrate on your talk. You look so stupid!" With apparent innocence I said: "Oh, you mean the way I look makes a difference on whether you will learn from me?" A total hush fell over the group. The lesson was taught, the props removed, and the discussion continued.

During the course of your teaching about the importance of looking like a missionary, you may want to try something along that order to get their attention. If the control does not come from the inside, the mission president will struggle the entire time your son or daughter serves. It certainly is no compliment to their level of maturity to have someone else remind them their hair needs to be cut, their shoes polished, their shirts ironed, their suits dry cleaned regularly, their dresses pressed, and their personal hygiene practiced. It was embarrassing to me and the missionary when I would have to encourage them to use deodorant or to brush their teeth or to use a dandruff shampoo. I know how difficult it is to "train up a child in the way he should go" (Proverbs 22:6), but it is not any easier for the mission president who has as many as 200 missionaries to deal with at any given time. Starting early and reinforcing your teaching regularly makes some of the basics become more a part of the normal routine. If young people begin in the mission field for the very first time to attend to themselves, the chances for slipping back are greatly increased.

Some of our young people seem to pride themselves in how sloppy they can look at church without the bishop saying something. Unless required by the bishop, some young priests do not even wear a tie to bless the sacrament. What a shock to their system to go from never wearing a tie to having one on sixteen hours a day, seven days a week. I am not suggesting that they wear a suit and tie to school but that they take some personal pride in the way they look and that they wear appropriate missionary attire as much as possible before going to the MTC.

Teen years are difficult at best. Sorting out feelings they have never encountered, seeing how to act in public, learning how to interact with adults, establishing proper relations with the opposite sex, learning to withstand peer pressure, practicing intelligent, adultlike conversation, learning to feel and recognize the Spirit, developing a stronger testimony, and many more such items are not things to be mastered overnight. But ignoring them or openly violating proper conduct only aggravates an already difficult experience.

At times it seems next to impossible to get teenagers to sit down and reason. If we give up easily, they get the idea all they have to do is act "stupid" and we'll leave them alone. If they know we are serious and genuinely interested in helping them avoid some embarrassing times, they may be more willing to listen. They may say things calculated to make you mad or hurt your feelings. Things like "this is stupid," "this is boring," or "get a life" are not unheard of. If you refuse to react to their bait, they often are at a loss on where to go next because their initial reaction has always worked. I hope you don't have those kinds of children—but somebody must because I sure met a bunch of them as missionaries in the mission field!

Although swearing may be just another "form of speech" among the young, one slip in the mission field causes untold embarrassment to the missionary, his companion, the investigators, and the members. To stop swearing the afternoon of the farewell almost guarantees problems later on when the normal stress of a mission goes far beyond anything they have ever experienced. Somehow, we have got to get their attention earlier and more seriously about swearing. Whether we hold family home evenings, one-on-one interviews, have a system of fines and rewards, or just appeal to their sense of propriety, whatever gains can be made will greatly reduce your missionary's adjustment in the missionary field.

For many, being a teenager is synonymous with being obnoxious. Because learning to express yourself intelligently is difficult, many take what they consider to be the "easy route" and act silly or "nerdy." Instead of judging them harshly, try understanding their behavior as a defense mechanism to avoid the embarrassment of not knowing what to say or how to say it. If you will put your arm around them and show them the correct way, you may be pleasantly surprised at how they respond.

Learning to teach and discipline the Lord's way is infinitely more successful and enjoyable than trying to invent a better way ourselves. Let us review six principles the Lord uses to discipline. They are found in Doctrine and Covenants 95. In verse 1, the Lord reveals: "Verily, thus saith the Lord unto you whom I love, and whom I love I also chasten. . . ." The controlling factor in discipline is the spirit in which it is given. If you cannot discipline in love, do not discipline! This is so important there is really no need to go further unless this one is followed. I remember a number of years ago when two of our little boys were upstairs in the family room really going at it. My wife came into the living room where I was apparently reading the newspaper. She asked if I would attend to the fight between the boys. I assured her I would. Without her observing, I had tried several times to go upstairs. Each time I felt anger well up inside to the point I knew I was not going in the spirit of love. I returned to my newspaper not to read or even look at the words but to pray and get the proper spirit so I could help the boys.

The second principle is also found in the first verse of Doctrine and Covenants 95: ". . . I also chasten that their sins may be forgiven . . . ." What is the purpose behind the discipline? Has someone dared to defy the authority of "almighty dad"? Are you disciplining because someone has dared to talk back to you? Are you really disciplining because you can see, unless corrected, their behavior will lead to serious problems later in life? Since every action has a consequence associated with it (either good or bad), part of our problem comes in our being able to know the consequences of our own and others' actions. Part of discipline is to truly want to save your child from the negative consequences that inescapably follow violation of the Lord's directives.

The third principle is taught in the conclusion of that same first verse: ". . . for with the chastisement I prepare a way for their deliverance in all things out of temptations, and I have loved you. . . . " Sometimes when we catch a child with his or her hand in the cookie jar, we instinctively slam the lid on the hand. A deer, which normally flees from the hunter will attack if cornered. A child who normally accepts discipline will defiantly oppose you if cornered. The Lord wisely advised us to prepare a way for them to escape, a way to save face, a way to let off steam before being disciplined.

In the example cited previously about our two boys fighting, my wife became frustrated at my apparent lack of action. She stormed upstairs, separated the boys, and sent each to his room. Then she came down the stairs and confronted me with what she viewed as a lack of support. I asked her if she had solved the problem. She confessed all she had really accomplished was to stop the fighting. We both realized the boys had not learned how to get along. They did not, at that time, like each other, and they did not have a greater respect for their mother based on her handling of the situation. In frustration she asked what I wanted her to do. I told her to alert me the next time the problem arose then go lock herself in our bedroom and turn up the stereo so she couldn't hear them.

The Lord seems to have a way of helping us learn lessons. It was only a day or two later the exact same scene was reenacted. As per the plan, my wife told me the boys were fighting—a fact that had not entirely escaped my notice. She left for the bedroom. Three or four times I started up the stairs trying to figure a way of stopping the fighting, teaching a lesson, and strengthening our relationship.

Finally, after a few more tense minutes and a lot of prayer, I thought I had a solution. I went to the entry of the family room. Immediately there was silence. The boys already knew they were doing wrong. They expected me to light into them with some kind of painful punishment. Instead I joined them on the floor.

We had assumed they knew what the problem was—a bad assumption. Following principle number four found in verse 3, which states: "For ye have sinned against me a very grievous sin, in that ye have . . . " The Lord took the time to definitely describe the sin. He did not leave them to wonder what they had done wrong. I sat there on the floor and explained that when the spirit of contention exists in a home, the Spirit of the Lord cannot. I further explained that although they had the right to fight if they wanted, they did not have the right to deprive everyone in the house of the Spirit.

Aided by a lot of Divine help, I moved on to principle number five, in which the Lord reexplains the desired behavior. He said: "Yea, verily I say unto you, I gave unto you a commandment that you should build a house, in the which house I design to endow those whom I have chosen with power from on high. . . ." Not leaving to chance that they understood how to act and why they are to get along, I taught them the principle of harmony in the home and the attendant rewards. Things were going pretty well. I kept praying a lot for continued assistance. After I had completed my teaching, I realized that there was one more step the Lord took. He helped them!

In verse 14 is recorded principle number six: "Therefore, let it be built after the manner which I shall show unto three of you . . . ." We did some fun role playing for the next few minutes. I would pose a situation and have them role play the "wrong way" and the "right way" to act. We acted out a half-a-dozen situations with their enthusiasm growing with each case. At the end I asked if they loved each other. They answered in the affirmative. I suggested that a mutual hug might cement the relationship. They readily complied. I asked if they still loved me. They both gave me a big hug as a demonstration of their love. I roughed up their hair and got up to leave. I got just to the entry way when my oldest son called after me, "Dad." For a minute I thought I had failed again. He continued, "Thanks, that was really fun!" I knew then, like I had never realized before, the power that comes from doing things the Lord's way.

My wife asked me how it went. I suggested she go talk to the boys. She came down from upstairs a few minutes later with a puzzled look on her face. "What did you do?" she asked. "Oh, nothing," I replied, "I just tried disciplining the Lord's way." Wouldn't it be nice if I could report that the boys have never fought since? I can't. Wouldn't it be great if I could truthfully say I have learned how to discipline the Lord's way in every situation? I can't. But from that one instance, I can testify how wonderful everyone feels when discipline is administered the Lord's way.

Learning how to do things "the Lord's way" is a lifetime pursuit. None of us have been perfect parents from the very start. There have been and will continue to be mistakes made and alterations made in our method of doing things. But if we constantly seek to discover and apply the Lord's way, we will find ourselves making fewer and fewer mistakes in the most common situations. Will we ever completely perfect ourselves in this life? No, but the process leading to perfection is rewarding and fun.

If prior experiences have soured your desire to help your children overcome undesirable traits, try again. We fail only if we refuse to try again. The Lord wants better prepared missionaries more than you and I want better behaved children. With his help we will eventually find a way to accomplish both our goals.

6

OVERCOMING GOLIATHS—PHYSICAL AND EMOTIONAL

FOR MANY YEARS PARENTS have viewed a mission as not only a time their children could serve the Lord but also as an easy method of helping them overcome their most serious defects. On March 4, 1993, the First Presidency issued a letter to priesthood leaders outlining the purpose for missions and the minimum qualifications a young man or young woman must meet before being recommended. I am not authorized to copy that letter for you. If you are unfamiliar with its contents, contact your bishop or branch president and ask him to discuss it with you. If your son or daughter has not had it reviewed in detail, request the bishop or branch president take the time to inform him or her. It is grossly unfair to have the criteria for service so plainly spelled out for both youth and adults by the First Presidency only to find the letter ending up in some file unused and not emphasized. In the missionary preparation classes I teach at Brigham Young University, well over 70 percent of the students report they have never heard of the letter.

Some of the general areas of the letter are certainly broad enough to consider. Missions are wonderful experiences if the missionary is prepared, focused, and motivated. Missionaries face rejection many times each day. If premissionaries do not develop personal skills in dealing with rejection, they will find themselves trying to work themselves out of a deep depression. Part of the role parents can play is to teach them strategies for coping with rejection. When a young person firmly understands people are rejecting the Savior and his message rather than the messenger personally, it makes coping easier. We are almost guaranteeing failure if we neglect to forewarn our children that the vast majority of people they meet will reject them as missionaries. The Lord outlined this rejection. He said: "And when the times of the Gentiles is come in, a light shall break forth among them that sit in darkness, and it shall be the fullness of my gospel; But *they receive it not*; for they perceive not the light, and they turn their hearts from me because of the precepts of men" (D&C 45:28-29; emphasis added).

When a young man or young woman develops unacceptable emotional responses to frustration, they put in jeopardy their opportunity to serve a mission. Beating up a companion who makes a mistake or merely disagrees with your son or daughter is simply not an acceptable response. Punching holes in the walls, leaving in a huff, sulking, pouting, and throwing temper tantrums just cannot be tolerated in the mission field. Almost all of us had some these "Goliaths" to overcome when we were young. Many young people realize their behavior is unacceptable but are at a loss as to how to overcome it. In a nonconfrontational setting, without attacking them verbally, try to give some suggestions that either you or someone you know may have successfully used. One of Satan's most effective tools is to "divide and conquer." Everyone seems to believe he or she is the only one who doesn't have his or her act totally together. When my son learned through a bedtime story that I too had struggled to be accepted during junior high school, it was like a huge burden had been lifted off his shoulders. We joked and laughed about how to deal with frustrations that are pretty common to early teens. When he could see I was not condemning him, he opened up and talked freely about his pent-up feelings of anger and isolation. Since that time we have enjoyed many such talks. Is he perfectly adjusted? Not by a long shot. But he is handling situations in a more acceptable way.

With violence such an all-pervasive influence, people throughout the world seem to be ringing their hands wondering what to do and what has gone wrong. As Latter-day Saints we are not exempted. More often than not, the overt signs of aggression are manifested in flaring tempers, shouting matches, or thunderous confrontations. When a parent realizes a son or daughter has no fuse whatsoever on his or her temper, what can be done? Ignoring it because "it is a long-standing family trait" is not helpful. Almost always the person feels terrible after an uncontrolled outburst. In a calm, quiet moment, it may be helpful to point the child in the right direction to overcome the problem.

You may be saying: "I don't have all the answers myself, but here are some tactics that may work." In dealing with not only temper but any other "Goliath," the Lord gives the following, reassuring counsel: "And if men come unto me I will show unto them their weakness. *I give unto men weakness* that they may be humble; and my grace is sufficient for all men that humble themselves before me; for if they humble themselves before me, and have faith in me, then will I make weak things become strong unto them" (Ether 12:27; emphasis added). Does that actually mean the Lord gives us weaknesses? That is what he said. But he did not say we must go to the grave with the weakness or spend a lifetime overcoming it. He did promise he would make areas that were formerly weaknesses become some of our strongest points on the condition we come unto him. Teach children to turn to God in times of stress and trial. Humbly, in faith, ask for his help and watch those "Goliaths" be conquered as surely as David of old eliminated his foe.

If mood swings are uncontrolled and threatening to either the person or others, they must be controlled before he or she will be permitted to serve. Putting yourself in the position of either the companion or the mission president, it becomes obvious why emotional stability is a must for those called to serve.

In a world where sin and corruption are not only made to look like normal, acceptable lifestyles, even desirable, is it any wonder our children need to understand the principle of worthiness. It was a rare missionary indeed who had not fallen short in one area or another. Some had problems with inactivity in the Church. Some had dealt with Word of Wisdom violations. Others suffered the remorse of breaking the moral code. Still others had problems with stealing, pornography, profanity, or drugs. I wish there was a surefire method of helping our youth avoid those pitfalls.

Perhaps we need to be more graphic and open in describing the suffering that will come to them *in spite of their repentance*. Too many young people have the mistaken idea repentance consists of a few prayers, a slap on the wrists by the bishop, and a short period of probation. Too bad they can't be photo-reduced to the size of a postage stamp and allowed to sit in an interview between a not-fully-repentant missionary and a mission president. Some of the most bitter suffering I have ever witnessed was experienced by missionaries who thought they could teach something they did not live. To their credit, most of them survived. Honestly, there were those who could not gain sufficient inner peace to enable them to complete their missions. They returned home to complete the repentance process. Regrettably, some of them never returned to complete their missions. Repentance takes time. Lack of complete repentance almost insures Satan's success in using flashbacks in the mission field. In a world where denying or avoiding consequences associated with behavior is the norm, it is increasingly difficult to help young people understand that there is a consequence for every action.

No one likes to watch people suffer, but I become more convinced every day we are not doing our children a favor by shielding them from the consequences of their own poor choices. A hundred times better to have them go through the complete repentance process before their missions than to postpone it until they are required to use the Lord's time to repent. It seems one of Satan's tactics used most frequently on missionaries is "the flashback." Everything they have ever done or said or thought is thrown back in their face in a devilish attempt to convince them they cannot be successful as missionaries. If the repentance process has been thorough and successfully completed, they will be able to command Satan to "get thee behind me," and he will obey. If they are not sure they have been totally honest in repenting, that same Satanic pressure crushes them.

Encourage, in the strongest language possible, every young man and young woman to take care of everything out of order in the past before the recommendation forms are submitted. What a powerful difference when worthy, prepared missionaries arrive having experienced firsthand the cleansing effects of the Atonement.

If the bishop or stake president determines that a waiting period is necessary before your son or daughter is ready to serve, accept his decision. No one needs to know the reason for the postponement. It could be a financial or medical preparation, or any other legitimate reason. When a missionary is returned from the field (which they will be if they have not been honest with their priesthood leaders), it is like a scarlet letter emblazoned on their forehead. By encouraging them to be totally honest before submitting their papers, help them avoid the terrible embarrassment of having to return home to complete the repentance process.

Missions are hard, physical experiences. From the outside it would seems relatively easy to get eight hours of sleep a night and just sit and talk to people about the gospel. However, there are many factors contributing to the physical difficulty of a mission. I will mention only a few. At home you, the parents, probably purchase the food, fix meals, do the laundry, clean the house, do the dishes, give the wake-up calls, and control disagreements between children. In the mission (unless you are really unusual!) you will not be accompanying your child. The responsibility shifts to his or her shoulders.

The easiest thing to do is take the easy way out—junk food. To the young this hardly sounds like a bad choice.

To those who have been around for awhile we note that junk food gives us a fast start but does not have the sustaining power of a good, well-balanced meal. So instead of eating breakfast they eat a sweet roll. Instead of going until lunch, they stop for a candy bar and soda water. Instead of a good lunch they stop for a hamburger at a fast-food restaurant. Instead of being sustained until dinnertime, they stop for a midafternoon snack of more junk food. By dinnertime their system is clogged so they pass up the nutritious food. The evening snack is often more junk food. Before too long the system starts to rebel. Diseases the healthy body can ward off find place in the run-down body. Not wanting to slow up the work, they continue the pace even though they can feel their health sliding. Before long a visit to the doctor or the hospital is necessary to get drugs to help the normal immune system (now weakened from abuse) fight the disease. The cycle is vicious and never ending.

If your son or daughter is prone to "catch every bug in the area," serious efforts should be made to build up the immune system before he or she enters the mission field. Without a knowledge of menus and cooking, young people do not know how to budget the limited resources provided monthly for necessities, which rapidly disappear. Although they look at the situation with some humor, it was always disturbing to me to discover missionaries who had been living on rice for the last two weeks of the month because of poor planning.

Normally the apartments where the missionaries are housed are adequate although not palatial. Even the best apartment becomes an epidemic waiting to happen when missionaries do not take the time to clean the sink, scrub the inside of the refrigerator, disinfect the shower and wash down the walls. During our quarterly inspections it was appalling to see how quickly some apartments could degenerate into a candidate for condemnation by the Health Services. Unless the parents take time to emphasize and demonstrate the importance of cleanliness, it is a losing battle for a mission president.

Over and over we emphasized "when the messenger goes down, the message does not get delivered." Unwashed clothing is disgusting to smell, offensive to look at, and wears out faster. Laundering does not have to take extra time to be done properly. Although we tried, at zone conferences, to reinforce proper laundry techniques, it was evident that some missionaries did not have an adequate base to build on. We spent many hours doing teaching which could have been done more effectively at home.

Although we feel concern for those young people who are seriously impaired physically, mentally, or emotionally, a little serious thought on your part will lead you to the conclusion that other means of service might be preferable. It was frustrating to receive a letter from concerned parents demanding a change in their missionary's companion. Little concern was voiced for the sons or daughters of other parents who would have to shoulder the burden of the troubled companion. One missionary reported during his exit testimony that he had served with twenty-four companions. An average of one a month! He looked at the situation as his having helped all those missionaries. In reality, one month was all his companions could endure. Although many lessons in patience and kindness can be learned from troubled missionaries, there is a limit to the value when contrasted with the Lord's work that went undone.

If the premissionary cannot or will not learn to solve problems with brothers and sisters, he or she is sentencing himself or herself to a lot of frustration when assigned to live with three other elders or sisters who are not so willing to tolerate childishness. Feigned illness, chronic headaches, frequent trips to the counselor, and daily mounting frustrations result from failure to prepare to serve with all one's heart, might, mind, and strength.

Too much experience in immoral areas makes it difficult to stay focused on the work when confronted with scenes that constantly remind the missionary of an immoral past. So difficult is the challenge to overcome those problems that certain teenage experiences require a minimum of one year from the latest transgression and as long as three years before papers can be processed.

Other areas put young people into a situation where the invitation to serve will not be extended. Circumstances dealing with fathering or giving birth to a child out of wedlock, participating in abortions, or teenage participation in homosexual experiences are serious, mission-threatening experiences. Please contact your priesthood leader if you have any question about what other danger areas are. What a terrible shame for young men or young women to disqualify themselves from missionary service before they are old enough to realize what they are doing. It may sound cruel to keep some young people home because of past problems, but from a mission president's perspective it is a blessing not even in disguise. When Goliath wins, everyone suffers. We are going to have to be much more direct in teaching our youth at a much earlier age if they are going to avoid the problems mentioned in the March 4, 1993, letter.

The real key, however, belongs only partly to the

parents. Until the young people wake up and join the battle, we will see increasing numbers of them forfeit the unparalleled privilege to which they were foreordained before the world ever was. Every David has a Goliath and every Goliath can be overcome. Those "David's" who went unprepared into their "Valley of Elah" and were consequently slain by Goliath are never mentioned in the Scriptures. I have unlimited confidence in the Brethren's wisdom in setting the guidelines for worthy service. Rather than try to rewrite the rules, teach your children to obey the rules so there will not be a question when their time for service comes.

7

········

HELP ME RISE

IT IS NOT UNCOMMON TO WELCOME a young missionary into the field who is shocked to discover that missionary work is difficult. Some have been told by parents or older brothers and sisters that people love the missionaries, feed them, look up to them, and do wonderful things for them. All of those things are true. However, there is another part to missionary life which is much more cruel and harsh. People are rude to missionaries, they say mean things to them, they frequently reject them, they try to entrap them into fruitless verbal battles, some try to injure them physically all under the guise of "doing God a favor."

If you really want to help your children prepare, let them see both sides of missionary life. Talk with them about how difficult it is to keep going when nothing seems to be going right. Work with them at home helping them find creative ways of solving problems. When missionaries try a single approach to get the ward members involved and it doesn't work, what is their reaction? Do they just throw up their hands in frustrated despair? The missionaries who have been prepared by patient, concerned parents take a step back, reevaluate the situation and come at the problem from a different direction. If the second try doesn't work, no problem, they have another dozen approaches to try before they begin to become anxious.

Creativity and a stick-to-it attitude are two essential characteristics common to outstanding missionaries. If those attitudes have been fostered at home, missionary work becomes an enjoyable challenge. If they have not been learned at home, missionary work can be overwhelming and discouraging. So in addition to the multitude of other areas you need to help your missionary in, you can now add the role of "Master Motivator."

How can you, as a parent, help them develop a "never-say-die" attitude? Practice creating a "vision" for them. Describe in some detail, so they can visualize in their mind's eye, what a successful missionary looks like. Paint a word picture realistically describing goals, challenges, and rewards earned by faithful service. Point out the pitfalls, problems, and setbacks a missionary might encounter and possible ways of succeeding. There is a certain amount of excitement generated when young people finally catch the vision of what can be. If we are failing in one area of parenting, it would probably be in our ability to create a clear enough vision in the minds of our children to arm them against the subtle temptations of Satan. The adversary makes everything look so good. When we fail to neutralize his influence by placing before them that which is even more desirable, they often partake of the forbidden. Too late they discover how really bitter the consequences of sin are.

In a world where they are constantly told what they cannot do, it is difficult for them to avoid placing an artificial ceiling on their accomplishments. For example, it was not uncommon to hear a missionary say:

"President, I just can't memorize scripture." They were so pathetic in their plea for understanding, it was tempting to excuse them from scripture memorization. Knowing the confidence which comes as their familiarity with the Scriptures increases, I would always require the memorization. Almost without exception, when they had memorized the "pass off" scriptures, they would proudly report how good it felt. What may have seemed like a cold, heartless refusal to consider their plight turned out to be the greatest blessing they had received.

Many years ago I heard a saying, the author of which I do not know, that has really helped me: "Treat a man like he is and he will forever remain on that level. But treat him like he can become and he will rise to meet your aspirations." I really believe it. In our attempt to be compassionate, we settle for mediocrity. Using a broader perspective, our compassion may cost young missionaries some times of regret and embarrassment in the mission field. Demand excellence and let them rise to that level.

I certainly am not suggesting we impose impossible demands. However, artificially self-imposed, low ceilings do not prepare missionaries. Years ago I was teaching an adult education class in Raleigh, North Carolina. At our first meeting I made the comment that before the year was over they could all easily have more than 500 verses at their immediate recall. The incredulous looks signaled their disbelief. One young married man decided to prove me wrong. He started putting verses on three-by-five recipe cards. He religiously followed my advice to look them over once a day for a week and then review them monthly. During our final class meeting, he asked if he could say something to the class. He said he had not believed for a minute my boastful challenge to memorize over 500 scriptures during the year. He publicly apologized for his lack of faith. He told about his experiment to prove me wrong. Through tears he admitted that I was wrong. He didn't just have 500 scriptures committed to memory—he had well over 1,000! I thought at the time I should have taken my own challenge more seriously.

A friendly challenge between family members could refresh such basics as the Thirteen Articles of Faith, the Presidents of the Church, the current Quorum of the Twelve Apostles, the names of the books in each volume of Scripture and the 100 most commonly used missionary scriptures. Obviously, the list could be greatly expanded. At first you may get that "you must be crazy" look. As you take one item a week starting during family home evening, they will rapidly catch the vision and, before long, surpass any efforts you make to keep up. Be prepared to have them lord over you their success. Their young minds are like sponges, adsorbing everything they hear. Why not direct that absorption to areas which are edifying and useful?

One of the more challenging areas a missionary faces is in getting along with the wide variety of people they meet. Companions and other missionaries are also in various stages of development—they are not all perfect! Members are not all carbon copies of your family at home. Investigators have spent a lifetime in a world so shockingly different from our own that it causes problems just trying to understand. If the missionary has not learned to get along with family members, small chance they will make the social adjustment to missionary work without some serious trauma.

Instead of demanding that they "stop acting like a teenager!" (which they are!), try teaching them how to act in an acceptable manner. Instead of just stopping the fight, teach them how to peacefully settle disputes. Instead of criticizing their acting obnoxious and offensive, role play acceptable behavior. Once you start thinking about the thousands of things you need to teach and skills they need to master, there is a serious shortage of Monday nights to accomplish all you need to do. It is so easy to stand back, raise our voices in loud condemnation of their behavior. It is much more difficult (and much more Christlike) to help them acquire the desirable traits.

One of the chief complaints I hear as I talk with young people is "My parents never really listen to me! All they want to do is lecture me." Are they correct? If not, it is at least their perception. Try sitting down (it might work better over a huge banana split!) and let them describe changes they think ought to be made to make your home more like the celestial kingdom. Ask clarifying questions but do not be accusatory. From your perspective, they may be the major cause of the problems they are identifying. It is very enlightening to "see things from my (your) child's point of view." You have plenty of time later to devise ways of helping them discover that indeed "I have met the enemy and he is me!" Ask for their suggestions as to how to solve the problems they have identified. To my great surprise, some of their suggestions are better than the ones I had considered! How could that be?

Sometimes they may be very vocal at pointing out the problems but be virtually silent when you ask for possible solutions. What a great teaching moment when they discover that identification of the problem is the easy part. Solving the problems takes intelligence and effort.

From many sad experiences, it became evident to me that some parents never allowed their children to make decisions on their own. It was frustrating and time consuming to interact with a missionary who could not make a decision and stick with it. At times I would say, "Elder, anything you decide is fine. Just decide and let me know and we'll make it work." They often could not make even the simplest decision.

Some things really don't make much difference. Should we bake a chocolate cake or an applesauce cake? Should we eat at McDonald's or Burger King? Should I wear the red dress or the blue one? By starting with our children when they are young, decision-making becomes easy and enjoyable. If they are not accustomed to making decisions, let them start with the easy ones. Teach them how to weigh the options, consider the consequences, and then go with their decision. It would be helpful, if the consequences are not too adverse, to allow them to make a few wrong decisions. After you have taken two hours longer and gone 50 miles further on this "shortcut," they may be open to some rational teaching.

Elder John H. Groberg of the First Quorum of Seventy gave some much needed advice on how to make a decision. He said:

> In the past I have tried to figure out whether I should go into business or into teaching or into the arts or whatever. As I have begun to proceed along one path, having more or less gathered what facts I could, I have found that if that decision was wrong or was taking me down the wrong path—not necessarily an

evil one, but one that was not right for me—without fail, the Lord has always let me know just this emphatically: "That is wrong; do not go that way. That is not for you!"

On the other hand, there may have been two or three ways that I could have gone, any one of which would have been right and would have been in the general area providing the experience and means whereby I could fulfill the mission that the Lord had in mind for me. Because he knows we need the growth, he generally does not point and say, "Open that door and go twelve yards in that direction; then turn right and go two miles . . . " But if it is wrong, he will let us know—we will feel it for sure. I am positive of that. So rather than saying, "I will not move until I have this burning in my heart," let us turn it around and say, "I will move, unless I feel it is wrong; and if it is wrong, then I will not do it." By eliminating all of these wrong courses, very quickly you will find yourself going in the direction that you ought to be going, and then you can receive the assurance: "Yes, I am going in the right direction. I am doing what my Father in Heaven wants me to do because I am not doing the things he does not want me to do." And you can know that for sure. That is part of the growth process and part of accomplishing what our Father in Heaven has in mind for us. (Elder John H. Groberg, "What Is Your Mission?" *Speeches of the Year, 1979*, Provo, UT: BYU Press, pp. 97-98).

As they mature closer to their missions, shift as many decisions onto their shoulders as possible—even some that normally are made by Mom or Dad are educational. "What shall we fix for dinner?" "Which car should we purchase and why?" "What can we do to help the neighbor who just lost his job?" Life provides ample opportunities to make decisions. It would be ideal if young missionaries could be totally comfortable in making difficult decisions before they reached the mission field.

Accepting full responsibility for one's actions is difficult even for adults. It seems the inclination to "pass the buck" came when Adam and Eve had their first personal priesthood interview after partaking of the fruit of the tree of knowledge of good and evil. You will recall how the interview began: "Adam, Where goest thou?" Realizing that his nakedness was apparent to the Father, he immediately passed the buck in two different directions: "The woman thou gavest me, and commandest that she should remain with me ... " In essence he said: "It is not my fault. It is either the woman's fault or Your fault. Don't forget, You gave me the woman and You commanded me to stay with her!" So the wife does not get too smug about Adam's response, we continue with the woman's personal priesthood interview. "And I, the Lord God, said unto the woman: What is this thing which thou hast done?" True to the pattern set by her husband, she responded: "The serpent beguiled me, and I did eat." She was in somewhat of a dilemma. She could not logically pass the buck back to her husband because he had just unloaded on her. So she shifted the blame to the serpent! (see Moses 4:7-25).

Perhaps these very human tendencies did not stop with Adam and Eve. Even adults still try to shift the responsibility for actions either to another person or maybe onto the environment. We even coined a term some years ago to describe this tendency: "The devil made me do it!" It was unusual and refreshing to hear a young man or young woman, when confronted with a violation of the rules, say: "I am in the wrong, president. What you would like me to do to make it right?" It almost required cardiac resuscitation it was so unexpected.

Practice and more practice after having taught the principle is the only way I know to help people begin accepting full responsibility. Occasionally, when one of our children is in the middle of making an excuse (passing the buck), we will stop and walk that child through the taking responsibility process. "Hold on. Let's see if we can make this easy. Sorry, Mom, I didn't mean to drop the milk all over the floor. Would you please help me clean it up?" We all laugh and clean up the milk. More importantly, a lesson has been taught and demonstrated. We need to be cautious not to speak down to our children or mock them as we teach. If we are sincere and helpful, they will sense the importance of the lesson.

There are so many other areas where an example is a more effective teacher than criticism, punishment, or ignoring—understanding scriptures, getting out of difficult social situations, controlling our tempers and tongues, recognizing answers to prayers, establishing good study habits, etc. Only a failure on our part to think about areas we wished we had been better prepared in as we moved into the mission field or the next stage of life will limit our ability to create learning situations that will help our children enter the mission field as polished Latter-day Saints.

8

STANDING ALONE IF NECESSARY

BEING ACCEPTED INTO THE GROUP seems to be such a powerful need during the growing- up years. Young men participate in activities contrary to their own beliefs and against the counsel of their parents in order to be with the "in group!" Young women too often sacrifice everything, even their virtue, to be numbered among the "popular group." What a shame that with some of the requirements for group acceptance comes the price tag of being disqualified for missionary service. Even the sound of the words "peer pressure" causes some parents to shudder. Is there anything we can do to counteract the negative influence of the peer group? Yes, and it isn't always difficult.

Perhaps in a family home evening setting a discussion could be held around Abraham Lincoln's famous statement: "When I do good I feel good and when I do bad I feel bad." Alma was a bit more graphic when he explained to his errant son, Corinthian: "Wickedness never was happiness" (Alma 41:10). As you openly discuss with your children the consequences of sin, you will be reminding them of principles they have been taught long ago by celestial teachers. What we do as we teach correct principles is only a reawakening.

Without condemning their friends who are choosing divergent lifestyles, we can share the promises of the Scriptures and the prophets of "the peaceable things—that which bringeth joy, that which bringeth life eternal" (D&C 42:61). It is always a source of amazement to me that the ones who are off the track seem to have more influence than those who are living right. The beginning of the battle between good and bad peer pressure is helping our children become aware of the problem. You could pose the question to them: "Why do you suppose the ones who are breaking the commandments seem to have more influence on the group than those who are trying to be good?" Their answers might be educational. Satan has always been successful in getting people to believe "everyone is doing it!" While teaching Seminary a friend of mine asked his students to estimate the number of fellow students in their class who broke the Word of Wisdom on a regular basis. He then asked in the same confidential questionnaire how many of them broke the Word of Wisdom on a regular basis. The findings were instructive. These students surmised that 80 percent or more of their classmates regularly broke the Word of Wisdom. The second question revealed that less than 20 percent actually admitted breaking the Word of Wisdom. Why the discrepancy? One could argue the violators were not being honest. Could it also possibly be the number of violators was not as great as Satan would have us believe?

Not everyone is "doing it" and not everyone is making fun of those who are trying to live right. Recent surveys by nationally known organizations reveal that many more teens are choosing to live chaste lives than the media would have us believe. With a little work we can create a vision of the real results of sin entirely different than the one Satan paints. Every ward and branch has examples of the hurt, pain, and destroyed lives resulting from infidelity and divorce. Unfortunately, your children will know more about the details of a divorce or unfaithfulness than you ever believed possible. Far from recommending we involve our children in the circles of gossip, I am suggesting we not shield them from the ever-present consequences of sinful behavior. Jacob, the great prophet/intellectual of the Book of Mormon taught: ". . . as ye look upon me as a teacher, it must needs be expedient that I teach you the consequences of sin" (2 Nephi 9:48). The adversary seems to have hoodwinked the entire world into believing there are no negative consequences for sin. Evidence abounds on every hand to see why the Lord calls Satan "a liar from the beginning" (D&C 93:25). Unless we identify irrefutable evidence documenting the negative effects of sin, the adversary continues to declare there aren't any. Only within the last few years have the tobacco company spokesmen stopped boldly denying any connection between smoking and cancer. The evidence became undeniable. Until then, they promoted their wares with total disregard to the health of their victims.

Not all the powerful leaders within your children's groups are perverts. Help your children identify with Captain Moroni or Helaman and the 2,000 Stripling Warriors. Let them know they can make the difference in their social settings. Armed with your teachings and a dose of parental support, they may find themselves pleasantly surprised at how much of a rallying point they can become for the cause of righteousness. Prepare them also for the teasing and snide remarks that will undoubtedly follow from those who recognize what they are doing is wrong but seem content to take the easy path to self-destruction.

While we were serving our mission in California, our teenage son was struggling to find good friends. He complained that the parties his friends went to violated every standard he knew to be right. He needed friends. We suggested he throw a party or two at the mission home. Rather than the normal "get a video, pop some popcorn, and watch" party, we helped him come up with some fun games. After much prompting and a lot of reassuring encouragement, he scheduled the party. A half hour before the designated beginning, he was sure no one would come. To his great surprise, everybody came! The party was a smashing success. He became an instant nominee for the "Party Thrower of the Year" award. The price we paid thereafter was his insatiable thirst for parties. We knew when the parties were at our home, we could help control the activities. He found, much to his amazement, there were a lot of young people who wanted to have a good fun party where everyone could remember the end of the party. As he gained confidence, his sphere of influence expanded from his own little group to the ward and eventually he began to make inroads into the high school. Perfect, he is not. A powerful leader, he is.

Sometimes we expect our children to do things which seem easy for us but go far beyond their current level of understanding. We can start by not assuming they will automatically be good or innately know how to be a leader in their social group. We can follow up by teaching them the "how's" of sociability. How do they meet new people; how do they carry a conversation;

how do they steer the activity or conversation away from undesirable areas?

Unfortunately, there are those who are "popular," "loud," and "persuasive" who can and do influence many good children into forbidden paths. Since they are not within your stewardship, your ability to control them is limited. Therefore we must be more aggressive in helping our children learn to stand alone, if necessary. Providing an accepting home environment gives our children a place to turn when the world turns cold and cruel. Perhaps they may even act a bit silly or unrestrained around home but it could be because they are so inhibited at school. If we continually reinforce their self-worth, it is easier for them to shrug off the cutting comments of the less disciplined.

No one likes to be called hurtful names. Teaching our children to evaluate the merit of the name and the motivation for the person calling them names could help them avoid overreacting. When another son came home with hurt feelings because some thoughtless student had called him "weirdo," it was a satisfying experience to turn with him to the Scriptures and reassure him who he is and what lies ahead for him. We got a good laugh as we read the Lord's answer to Moroni when he became concerned about the possible future response of the "Gentiles" when the Book of Mormon was presented to them. The Lord said: "Fools mock, but they shall mourn" (Ether 12:26). Unfortunately, our son remembered too well the Lord's response and used it several times on some of his mocking friends! Actually, what could have been a tense social situation became a laughing matter as his friends realized how childish name-calling really is.

There are enough good young men and women who can see through the shallowness of the world's "large and spacious building" that our children do not need be socially isolated. Sometimes the less bold need a "Captain Moroni" to hold up the Standard of Liberty so they can rally around it. As they gain experience and confidence, it will become increasingly easier for them to walk away from the detractors.

It would be wonderful if the end of high school signaled the end of the peer pressure. However, there seems to be a few missionaries who find diligent service too demanding. Rather than rolling up their sleeves and redoubling their effort, they want to slack off and ride out the two years exerting minimal effort. Unfortunately, they are not comfortable in being slothful alone—it would be too embarrassing if everyone else were diligent. They want to spread their poison to other missionaries. It is difficult as a mission president to constantly stay on top of those who decide to take a more casual approach. If your missionary does not take some initiative, he may find pressure being exerted by the casual missionary to kick back and relax. If he has successfully learned how to resist peer pressure at home during those turbulent high school years, resisting pressure to waste the Lord's time will be simple. If he has not learned before his mission, it is very difficult to stand against the lazy missionary who usually has seniority.

The flip side of the "resisting peer pressure" coin is helping our children be sensitive enough not to offend others. If we overteach the principle of standing independent, the overreaction is almost as painful as the issue we are trying to help them avoid. When young people develop the attitude that their personal wants take precedence over everyone else's, they becomes difficult to work around. Often their attitude is manifest by statements like: "If people don't like the way I act, that is their problem." Leaving a meeting before the closing prayer, coming late to meetings, not showing up at all when commitments have been made, all are manifestations of an attitude in need of softening.

Convincing young people of the need for increased sensitivity is in many respects more difficult than teaching them to stand against peer pressure. Simulated experiences discussed during family home evening help increase the awareness level. We have tried setting up methods of alerting each other when we are bordering on social insensitivity. It is a constant battle but very rewarding when children start to realize they have a responsibility to those around them. If you can help them see the need to cooperate and be serious, role playing different social situations provides ample opportunities to fine-tune skills they are often embarrassed to admit they lack.

As a professional teacher I have noticed students will use a multitude of diversionary tactics to avoid confronting a deficiency or weakness. It is pathetically appalling how many students cannot locate a simple scripture reference—not because they really cannot find it, but because they don't have enough confidence in their ability to read before the class. Classroom disruption is often associated with discussions which come too close to areas of needed improvement. Rather than admit they need to shape up their lives, they will do something requiring the teacher to break the line of reasoning in order to control their disruption. When the depth of a discussion goes beyond what they are capable of easily understanding, they may put their head down and either go to sleep or pretend to be asleep.

In a family discussion, annoying mannerisms calculated to aggravate you may signal sensitive areas where your child feels the consequences of unacceptable behavior would be less painful than the embarrassment resulting from failure. In a loving, accepting, noncondemning environment, talk through reasons for his or her socially unacceptable behavior. Provide opportunities to demonstrate proficiency in areas used frequently in missionary work. Family scripture reading quickly reveals any hesitancy or inability to read. Family home evening lessons point out weakness in many areas of teaching. Family prayer draws attention to lack of familiarity with prayer language and ease in vocally praying. Father/mother interviews with the child magnifies a child's lack of confidence in meeting an adult eye to eye. It also provides opportunity to detect areas of needed improvement in clearly expressing himself or herself to an adult. The opportunities are endless if we are not willing to be diverted by smoke-screen tactics.

It is heartbreaking to see a young missionary who has never learned to stand against the tide of popular opinion. We can have an influence if we will recognize the challenge and seek the help of the Lord in finding creative ways of teaching our children the basics of relying upon Heavenly Father. If they seem a little reluctant at first, do not get discouraged. Whatever gains you make will pay huge dividends as they strengthen their resolve to "stand as a witness of God at all times and in all things, and in all places that they may be in, even until death" (Mosiah 18:9). It may be that one person cannot change the entire world—but, maybe they can. We must try to instill in our children that "can do" attitude common to all great people who really succeed. Do not let them become self-fulfilling prophecies of "I can't."

9

Control from Within

It doesn't require much imagination to see the problems created for a mission president when missionaries have not learned to control themselves. One of the most difficult concepts to teach children seems to be that they must learn to govern themselves. They must learn to evaluate the situation, draw upon the teachings of the Church and parents, weigh the consequences of the possible options, and make wise and correct decisions.

Too many parents apparently failed to teach or gave up in frustration when it came to preparing their children in some of the most basic areas, such as how to keep their rooms clean, how to do the laundry, how to do the dishes, how to follow through on chores they dislike, how to obey when no one is watching or checking up. These and many other lessons so vital to success as a missionary and also in life were left for the mission president and his wife to teach. No one is suggesting the challenge is easy. No one is throwing stones for failure on the part of the missionary to master these basic but vital skills. Could we be more effective if we systematically addressed areas most commonly deficient?

Failing to keep a clean room results in more companionship friction than we care to admit. If all of the missionaries are untidy, the problem does not come from irritations between the missionaries directly, it comes when the Spirit withdraws from the apartment and leaves them subject to the buffeting of Satan. How can you help teach cleanliness? First, do not assume your son or daughter knows how to keep the room straight. Maybe he or she does and maybe not. Eliminate any question by a little "on the job training." Go to the "war zone" but DO NOT CLEAN IT FOR YOUR CHILD! How will children ever learn if they know when it gets bad enough, you will rush in and rescue them? Have a set time for a "military inspection." We used to do that with our children and they loved it. We would make a game of cleaning up. Using the example set by the Lord in the creation of the earth, we would break the superordinate task (too big to handle) into smaller, more manageable tasks. Instead of "Clean up your room!" we would say: "Just bring all dirty clothes to the bedroom door. Do not do anything else, then come and report." Following the Lord's example of declaring each successfully completed task as "good," we would praise them for their accomplishment. As they stood at "attention" we would give them their next task: "Just hang up the clothes which do not require laundering." They would race off to complete that task and within seconds be back to "report." Praise, then another assignment. "Now, pick up the books and papers which are laying around. Organize them and put them in the appropriate place." Off they would go, enthused at making work such a fun game. Back for a report, praise, and yet another assignment. "Now change the sheets on your bed and make the bed so it will pass military inspection."

They liked this part best because "military inspection" meant dad would flip a quarter on the bed. If it bounced, the bed was properly made. If it did not, they had to remake the bed. Report, praise, assignment. "Dust the dresser, shelves, window sills, desks, etc." Report, praise, assignment. "Vacuum floors." As they completed the task, a visual inspection was made by the company commander (Dad) and, if all went as planned, the verdict "Very Good" was pronounced. In one-tenth the time it normally takes, the Saturday's chores were done and we all felt better about playing for a while. Work does not have to be drudgery unless we make it that way.

The previously described method may not work for you without some modifications. But it is a "must" to teach children how to have a house of order. Doing the dishes is actually easier than cleaning the house. All that is required is teaching the philosophy that the meal is not over until the table is cleared, the dishes done, and the floor swept. "No, you can't be excused to go to ball practice until the meal is complete." The most challenging part of dishes is consistent follow-through. In far too many Latter-day Saint homes, Mom has been reduced to the domestic slave. Although you (the mother or father) may view that as part of your role, you are doing your son or daughter a grave disservice unless you plan on accompanying them on their mission. To the young man who sees "dishes and housework" as a woman's job, I extend my condolences, not only to him but to his future wife and also to his missionary companions. That kind of a chauvinistic attitude is destined to bring grief into situations where joy should prevail.

Again based on our experience in our personal lives as well as the hundreds of missionaries we observed, a more diligent effort at home pays great dividends in the mission field. Don't get discouraged. If you fail, who do you think is going to have to continue the educational process in the mission field? Right, companions and mission leaders, both of whom are infinitely too busy with really important jobs to baby-sit a nineteen- to twenty-year-old who hasn't learned to work. The bottom-line key is to help young people realize they must assume responsibility for their own behavior. Unfortunately, they have grown up in a world which fosters irresponsibility: something for nothing, the world owes me a living, do whatever I like and let others worry about the consequence, plus many more such ideas that will not be new to you.

In your quest to help them grow up, there needs to be a balance between helping them succeed and letting them suffer the consequences of their behavior. If we did not exert some influence to keep them from hurting themselves, many would never live to mission age. However, to shield them from all consequences associated with their irresponsible behavior is an equally great disservice. Whenever they try to shift the responsibility for their behavior or decisions onto you, refuse to take it. "You made me fail that test!" How ridiculous! You didn't take the test for them, you are not enrolled in the class, you are not the one who failed to study, you are not the one who will be adversely impacted academically in the future because of their failure.

This generation has become notorious for laying "guilt trips" on parents and teachers. Frequently during interviews I would have to remind the missionary not to confess his or her companion's sins. Whenever I would ask what was wrong, the most frequent responses

71

started with "my companion . . . " If you give your son an assignment to "take out the garbage" and he fails to perform, every response will be an excuse attempting to justify unacceptable behavior. If we could help our children to accept blame when they fail as well as praise when they succeed, they would be much closer to missionary-caliber people. If the only time your children obey the family rules is when you are supervising them, they will be in trouble in the mission field. It is unreasonable to expect a mission president to give a "wake-up call" to 200 missionaries every day. If the missionaries do not strive to understand the rules and voluntarily obey them, the life of a mission president becomes impossible. Attitude towards rules should be taught at home. Are commandments restrictive, intended to curtail our fun and enjoyment of life? If that statement reflects our attitude, how can we expect our children to submit cheerfully to the many mission rules established by the General Authorities to help them be successful?

It is rewarding to sit down and explain the "why's" behind the family rules and the commandments from our Heavenly Father. Sometimes, however, they must learn to obey without a full understanding merely because they have faith in the lawgiver. It is not uncommon for young people to enter the mission field having been schooled in these principles and prepared to do whatever the "white handbook" says. Those who require everything in writing with supporting documentation from the Brethren suffer a lot of unnecessary frustration as they learn to bring their unruly wills into subjection to the Savior's chosen leaders.

Sometimes I wish I could just find the person responsible for introducing "excuses" and get rid of him.

Of course that "someone" is the adversary—the master excuse maker. It is a rare young man or young woman who readily assumes responsibility for all his or her mistakes. If money runs out before the end of the month, it is too easy to blame an unexpected flat on the bicycle. If a talk is not adequately prepared for sacrament meeting, there will generally be a "valid excuse" calculated to justify failure to prepare. It seems to be human nature to want to shift responsibility to someone else. Perhaps we try to avoid responsibility because we are not comfortable in accepting the blame. If the reason is that easy, practice with your premissionary until he or she can admit guilt, apologize for the inconvenience, and take whatever action is necessary to remedy the problem.

For some reason it seems equally difficult for a person to accept praise or compliments on something they do well. Teaching a child to humbly accept a compliment with a simple "Thank you" doesn't sound that difficult, but it is challenging. There seems to be resistance to giving praise to those who deserve it. Because we live in a competitive society, we tend to view everyone else's success as one less chance we have for success. It is difficult to change that thinking in the mission field. There are not a limited number of seats in the celestial kingdom. Everyone who qualifies can make it without lessening our chances. The art of giving praise is a dying art among the young. Maybe a family home evening or two practicing expressing love and thanks could produce dividends that will enrich an impoverished world.

Tearing others down, gossip, tale bearing, and sarcastic remarks also hurt the missionary and cause the partial withdrawal of the Spirit. "Everybody does it" is hardly a valid excuse. Looking at life through rose-colored glasses is not healthy either. With some additional practice we can teach our children to critically evaluate the situation without attacking the person or persons involved. It is a given that there will never come a time (before the Millennium!) that missionaries will always agree with everything a bishop or ward mission leader does. Our diversity contributes to our beauty. One of the many challenges we still face as parents is to get our children to be more tolerant with the weaknesses and differences of others. It is instructive to remember the Pharisees and Sadducees easily found fault in the sinless Son of God.

Too often, without our even being aware, we set ourselves up as the standard by which right and wrong are judged. If we like something, it must be good. If we dislike something, it must be bad. Much of what we see that is labeled "sin" in others is often no more than their different way of doing things. Fortunate is the missionary who has learned at home to "leave judgment alone with me [the Lord], for it is mine . . . " (D&C 82:23). The added burdens missionaries shoulder as they try to magnify someone else's office need not be burdensome if we can just teach them to magnify their own offices.

The items discussed in this chapter may seem impossible to accomplish. They may be unless we realize whose responsibility it is to master them. If you diligently try to help your missionary internalize these Christlike qualities and they refuse, the problem is not yours, but theirs. Even if you are only partially successful in one area, so much the better for those who must continue the teaching process where you left off.

A mission is a mutual effort by parents and mission leaders. It is not a "you guys" and "us guys" situation. If we refuse to become adversarial, miracles can and do happen in the lives of our missionaries. Be slow to criticize the mission president for not being able to do in a couple of months what you have been working on for years. With the help of the Lord and the willingness of the missionary, great changes will take place. Eventually they will stand and call you blessed for your untiring efforts to prepare them to serve valiantly.

10

WHO AM I?

As WE DIRECT OUR CHILDREN towards missionary service, we are often frustrated at their apparent lack of motivation to serve. Sometimes they lack motivation because there are problems with unworthiness. They throw up the smoke screen "I don't want to go" rather than say "I am not worthy to go." On other occasions young people turn their back on missionary service because they feel unprepared to go. They may have not been as serious about studying the gospel and memorizing scriptures as they should have been. Now faced with the prospects of their being embarrassed because of their failure, they opt to stay home. Many of these young people ridicule those who are preparing, calling a mission a "waste of time." It is an absolute certainty that those who are labeling missions as a "waste of time" have never served! Even the ones who have been away for two years under the guise of missionary service have never really served if they label it a "waste of time." We can help these young people by honestly identifying the reason for their attitude and work to overcome it.

However, another group really needs our help. These are faithful, worthy young people who have been knocked around by the world and told they are "worthless" or "no good" or "stupid" or "unqualified" or any other such term which strips them of self-esteem. I have been amused at a tactic used so successfully by Satan. Perhaps an analogy will clarify the point. In a basketball game, who does the opposing team double-team? Everyone knows the answer—the best person on our team. The one who, left unguarded, will make the basket, get the rebound, and hurt their chances for victory. They are almost unconcerned about the uncoordinated player who double dribbles the ball every time he or she gets it, or loses the ball out of bounds, or who could not hit the basket if the ball were magnetized. Why then does Satan double-team our young people while whispering in their ears they are no good, incompetent, and unworthy? The real question is "Why do our young people believe him?"

To arm you with what the prophets and other General Authorities are saying about today's youth, I am including a sampling of their statements:

CHOSEN YOUTH

> For nearly six thousand years, God has held you in reserve to make your appearance in the final days before the Second Coming of the Lord. . . . While our generation will be comparable in wickedness to the days of Noah, when the Lord cleansed the earth by flood, there is a major difference this time. It is that God has saved for the final inning some of his strongest children, who will help bear off the Kingdom triumphantly. And that is where you come in, for you are the generation that must be prepared to meet your God.

All through the ages the prophets have looked down through the corridors of time to our day. Billions of the deceased and those yet to be born have their eyes on us. Make no mistake about it—you are a marked generation. There has never been more expected of the faithful in such a short period of time as there is of us. Never before on the face of this earth have the forces of evil and the forces of good been as well organized. Now is the great day of the devil's power, with the greatest mass murderers of all time living among us. But now is also the great day of the Lord's power, with the greatest number ever of priesthood holders on the earth. And the showdown is fast approaching. (Ezra Taft Benson "In His Steps," in *Speeches of the Year, 1979*, Provo, UT: BYU Press, 1980, p. 59)

Never before in history has there lived a more valiant generation of youth. I am convinced the spirits of this generation were held to come forth at this important time in history. Their potential is unlimited (Victor L. Brown, "Is There Not a Cause?" *Ensign*, Nov. 1974, p. 104)

My dear friends, you are a royal generation. You were preserved to come to the earth in this time for a special purpose. Not just a few of you, but all of you. There are things for each of you to do that no one else can do as well as you. If you do not prepare to do them, they will not be done. Your mission is unique and distinctive for you. Please don't make another have to take your place. He or she can't do it as well as you can. If you will let Him, I testify that our Father in Heaven will walk with you through the journey of life and inspire you to know your special purpose here. (H. Burke Peterson, "Your Life Has a Purpose," *New Era*, May 1979, p. 5)

Tonight I would like to talk principally to the young men of the Aaronic Priesthood about the responsibility you have to live in such a way that you can be a good influence in your homes, whatever the conditions there may be, and so that you can qualify to do all the Lord expects of you during your lifetime.

Young men, I do not believe that you are here upon the earth at this time by accident. I believe you qualified in the premortal life to come into mortality at a time when great things would be required of you. I believe you demonstrated before you came here that you were capable of being trusted under unusually difficult circumstances—that you could measure up to the most difficult challenges. Don't misunderstand me. I don't suggest that you are inherently better than or superior to any of the other generations that have come to the earth. You do not automatically qualify for any more blessings or advantages than anyone else who has lived since the earth was created. You can go astray, become involved in transgression, and incur the judgments of God as readily as any who have preceded you here. In fact, you live in an environment in which it is probably as easy to disqualify yourselves in this way as any generation has ever experienced. But God trusts that you will not. He relies upon you to keep yourselves eligible to accomplish the monumental tasks that he expects you to achieve.

My beloved friends, you are the vanguard of the righteous spirits to be infused into the Church in the last days. Back beyond time, it was so determined, and you were prepared—before the foundations of the world—to help save others in the latter-day world.

You cannot keep that resplendent rendezvous if you become like the world! Make your righteous marks on the world instead of being spotted by the world.

Be true, now, to your emotions of long ago when, as the Lord set in motion His plan of Salvation and laid the foundation of this earth, "The morning stars sang together, and all the sons (and daughters) of God shouted for joy" (Job 38:7). (Elder Neal A. Maxwell, Young Adult Fireside on Temple Square, June 23, 1985)

The Lord has chosen a small number of choice spirits of Sons and Daughters out of all the creations of God, who are to inherit this earth, and the company of choice spirits have been kept in the Spirit World for 6000 years, to come forth in the last days, to stand in the flesh in the last dispensation of the fullness of times, to organize the Kingdom of God upon the earth, to build it up and to defend it . . . and to receive the eternal and everlasting Priesthood. (Wilford Woodruff, as cited in "Our Lineage," *Topical Outline to the Way to Perfection,* Sunday School manual, 1932 [Salt Lake City: Genealogical Society of Utah, n.d.], p. 4)

You our youth of today are among the most illustrious spirits to be born into mortality in any age of the World. Yours is a noble heritage and a wonderful opportunity. May you join in the refrain of the rallying song of youth today: "Holding aloft our colors, we march in the glorious dawn, O youth of the noble birthright, Carry on, Carry on, Carry on!" and be guided to fulfill your highest destiny. (Harold B. Lee, *Youth and the Church* [Salt Lake City: Deseret Book Co., 1970], p. 169)

Our young people are among the most blessed and favored of our Father's children. They are the nobility of heaven, a choice and chosen generation who have a divine destiny. Their spirits have been reserved to come forth in this day when the Gospel is on earth, and when the Lord needs valiant servants to carry on His great latter-day work.

May the Lord bless you, the youth of Zion, and keep you true to every covenant and obligation, cause you to walk in paths of light and truth, and preserve you for the great labors ahead. (Joseph Fielding Smith, in *Church News*, July 10, 1971, p. 14)

Perhaps we have overemphasized the "chosen" aspect of their calling without giving proper emphasis to the question "Chosen to do what?" They really are chosen to work harder, give more, sacrifice more than any generation before them. No wonder the adversary is making such a valiant attempt to derail them. If he can distort their self-esteem, either on the side of being too puffed up or on the side of low self-esteem, he can (at least temporarily) lessen their effectiveness.

They are called on missions to serve God. 1 John 4:8 states: "God is Love." In stating the two great commandments, the Savior said: "Thou shalt love the Lord thy God with all thy heart, and with all thy soul, and with all thy mind. This is the first and great commandment. And the second is like unto it, Thou shalt love thy neighbour as thyself" (Matthew 22:37–39). Perhaps fearing we might misinterpret his counsel to develop a healthy respect (love) for ourselves, he reiterates the command in these last days. In Doctrine and Covenants 112:11 the Lord states: "I know thy heart, and have heard thy prayers concerning thy brethren. Be not partial towards them in love above many others, but let thy love be for them as for thyself; and let thy love abound unto all men, and unto all who love my name."

Until young men or young women can learn to appreciate themselves, how can they adequately represent God? Until they successfully come to know who they are and what has been said about them, they will waste too much time worrying over their own standing before God while giving diminished service to Heavenly Father's other children. Perhaps as parents we should review with them Abraham 3:22–26 in conjunction with the preceding quotes. In helping Father Abraham understand who he was, Heavenly Father showed him a vision of the "many noble and great ones." We tend to think of strength and goodness as "them" and failure and weakness as "me." However, the Lord said: "And God saw these souls that they were good, and he stood in the midst of them, and he said: These I will make my rulers; for he stood among those that were spirits, and he saw that they were good; and he said unto me: Abraham, thou art one of them; thou wast chosen before thou wast born." Note carefully the Lord calls the noble and great ones "good" twice. Unless He is mistaken, we may be more advanced than we are willing to admit. Note again the Lord saw the "spirits" and the "souls" that they were good. The spirit represents our condition during pre-earth life. The soul is the spirit and the body combined (see D&C 88:15). So during the pre-earth life, mortality, and the post-earth life the One who never makes a mistake saw that we were "good." What a thrill to realize that in spite of all my weaknesses, the Lord sees me as I can become rather than the way I am right now. Keeping things in proper eternal perspective should help us avoid "getting down on ourselves."

What destroys self-esteem? Perhaps when our behavior falls short of our knowledge of what is expected, we look with a condemning eye at ourselves. While it is true that the "Lord cannot look upon sin with the least degree of allowance" (D&C 1:31), it is also true that allowance must be made for the sinner who is trying to be obedient. Joseph Smith taught:

> It is one evidence that men are unacquainted with the principles of godliness to behold the contraction of affectionate feelings and lack of charity in the world. The power and glory of godliness is spread out on a broad principle to throw out the mantle of charity. God does not look on sin with allowance, but when men have sinned, there must be allowance made for them.

> All the religious world is boasting of righteousness; it is the doctrine of the devil to retard the human mind, and hinder our progress, by filling us with self-righteousness. The nearer we get to our heavenly Father, the more we are disposed to look with

compassion on perishing souls; we feel that we want to take them upon our shoulders, and cast their sins behind our backs. My talk is intended for all this society; if you would have God have mercy on you, have mercy on one another. (*Teaching of the Prophet Joseph Smith*, pp. 240-41).

Realizing what the Lord has revealed about Satan's tactics helps us prepare ourselves and our children for the problems we will face as we consciously engage in activities which win people away from his kingdom. In his incomparable wisdom God said: "And it must needs be that the devil should tempt the children of men, or they could not be agents unto themselves; for if they never should have bitter they could not know the sweet" (D&C 29:39). It is no new revelation to us that Satan tempts all humankind. However, the Lord's account of Satan's relationship with the Saints puts a different light on what we are experiencing. He said: "Wherefore, he [Satan] maketh war with the saints of God, and encompasseth them round about" (D&C 76:29). We need to expect a virtual "war" when we join the Savior's crusade to save the souls of our brothers and sisters. "Encompass" means to completely encircle or envelop. There will not be an area where we and our children will not be buffeted. It would be less than prudent if we failed to alert our children to the increase in temptations they will face not only as they prepare to serve but also as they serve their missions. Make sure you emphasize the difference in intensity between "being tempted" and having "war" waged against them. As a mission president, one of the areas that caused the greatest disappointment was to watch missionaries fall prey to the subtle temptations of the adversary because they considered themselves immune from such temptations *because* they were missionaries. What a revelation they received as they learned that they were more the focus for the temptations, not less, *because* they were missionaries.

It is helpful to stand back from our present situation and view life as God sees it. If we take time to look at all the many things our children do well, we are lead to conclude they are only struggling in a relatively few areas. Try putting it into a school setting. If you took a test and scored between 95 and 99 out of 100, how would you feel? I'd feel great! Before I retired the test to an obscure box or the trash bin I would probably glance through and see which questions I missed. Should we do less with life? Our children are probably doing between 95 percent and 99 percent of what the Lord requires. Satan would have us believe there isn't any 95-99 percent. He wants us to dwell endlessly on the 1-5 percent where we still need improvement.

Although not attempting to minimize the necessity of perfecting ourselves, perhaps it would be more profitable if we remembered the Lord's description of those who go to the celestial kingdom. He said: "And they *shall* overcome all things" (D&C 76:60; emphasis added). The Prophet Joseph Smith confirmed that teaching when he taught:

When you climb up a ladder, you must begin at the bottom, and ascend step by step, until you arrive at the top; and so it is with the principles of the Gospel—you must begin with the first, and go on until you learn all the principles of exaltation. But it will be a great while after you have passed through the veil before you will have learned them. It is not all to be comprehended in this world; it will be a great work to learn our salvation and exaltation even beyond the grave (*Teachings of the Prophet Joseph Smith*, p. 348)

We can and should help our children identify and overcome self-defeating behavior, but in the same breath we should commend them on their present efforts. Nothing breeds success like success. Before we look at how far we have yet to go, it might be helpful to look at how far we have come. When all we do is focus on failure, it is easy to become discouraged and give up.

If you really want to help your children achieve their potential, avoid playing into the hands of the adversary. Remember during the recital of the creation, the Lord called each phase "good" in spite of its incompleteness. Remembering who we are and what our destiny is should make the task of training our children more manageable.

Notice the difference in people who focuses solely on their mistakes. Another failure at perfection becomes apparent and they are apt to say: "I knew I couldn't be perfect no matter how hard I tried!" Contrast that with people who understand that life is a test and that perfection is a process and not an event. They discover another area they need improvement in but humbly recognize their success in keeping most of the commandments of God. Armed with the confidence that they really can (with the help of the Lord) overcome weaknesses, they are likely to view challenges entirely differently from the first group. At eighty years of age, Caleb verbalized the "can do" spirit. He said: "Now therefore give me this mountain, whereof the LORD spake. . . . if so be the LORD *will be* with me, then I shall be able to drive them out, as the LORD said" (Joshua 14:12). He was facing fierce, godless nations. We are facing fierce, godless demons and habits. With the help of God, we can successfully overcome our weakness just as Caleb did his adversaries.

Probably as essential as any attitude we can help our children develop is the positive, obedient attitude which characterized the Savior. To the more obedient Nephites who were privileged to receive his ministrations as a resurrected being, the Savior explained: "Behold I have given unto you my gospel, and this is the gospel which I have given unto you—that I came into the world to do the will of my Father, because my Father sent me. And my Father sent me that I might be lifted up upon the cross" (3 Nephi 27:13-14). He came because he was commanded. He performed his mission because he was obedient. If we are determined to become like him, we use those two attitudes as a starting place for ourselves and teach them freely to our children.

HELPING YOUR MISSIONARY SERVE WITH HONOR

11
....

HELPING YOUR MISSIONARY DEAL
WITH HOMESICKNESS

IS YOUR SON OR DAUGHTER WIMPY because he or she experiences homesickness in the mission field? Not at all. If our experience is typical, almost every missionary has one or more of these experiences. The experience was so common we included it in the orientation the day the missionary arrived. We would say, "Let us tell you something that will probably happen any time between tonight and three or four months from now. You will wake up one morning, look at the ceiling and say to yourself, 'I am not cut out to be a missionary!' That is just as normal and expected as the sun coming up each morning. It is called 'homesickness.' It is not a terminal disease and can be overcome rather easily. Just admit you have got it; get on your knees and pray a little more earnestly; read the Scriptures with a lot more intensity, looking for counsel specifically for you; get outside yourself and start serving. Serve your companion—fix his breakfast, polish his shoes, iron her dress. Put on a smile and go out and find somebody to teach about the great plan of salvation. Stay out all day—even if you don't want to. When you come back at 9:30 p.m., you will be so dogged tired you will just flop into the chair. As you reflect on the way you feel, you will note the home-sickness is gone or just about gone. Continue each day living just one day at a time and soon you will forget you ever felt like throwing in the towel."

Sometimes just knowing that almost everyone has experienced the same thing your missionary is feeling makes all the difference in the world. If or when you get that letter hinting he or she is not cut out to be a missionary, write back discussing some of the ideas we will look at in this chapter. Generally by the time your missionary receives your letter, the crisis is past and everything is all right. If there are serious overtures about coming home, have your bishop or stake president contact the mission president.

Why would missionaries get homesick? Some have been away for a year or more at college. Should not that have cured them? Not necessarily. At college they could choose their classes, their friends, their extracurricular activities. They could spend some time alone, go to a movie, call home any time they wanted, date, drop classes or any of a hundred other freedoms they do not have in the mission field. As missionaries, they go where they are assigned, with someone they may actually not like. They are in a totally different environment, sometimes trying to speak a language they don't understand, eating food they prefer not to eat, adjusting to customs and cultures which are strange and new. They are asked to wear a white shirt and tie or a dress all day long, pray multiple times a day, read the Scriptures, stay with their companions, attend meetings, eliminate any romantic relationships with the opposite sex, adhere to a schedule which is new and demanding, and cope with the buffetings of Satan, which are stronger than anything they have ever experienced. And we wonder why they get overwhelmed!

Encourage them before they ever leave home to suspend judgment, for the first two or three months, about the mission, missionaries, missionary work, and their ability to succeed. Before they enter the MTC they will not understand what you are saying. In answer to their first homesick letter, you can remind them about the talk you had before they left.

If you are aware, as a parent, that most missionaries go through the feeling "overwhelmed" stage, you can write back and encourage them to discuss their feelings with their companion and other missionaries. The fact that others have gone through the same experience, and survived, is therapeutic.

In your letters help them set short-range goals. "Stay until the end of the month or until the next transfer so it won't severely impact the mission." The adversary has had years of experience on many thousands of missionaries in trying to wrongly convince them they cannot succeed. Unfortunately, he has been and continues to be altogether too successful. If one young man or woman comes home early because of homesickness, it is a tragedy. His primary tactic seems to be to get them to focus on how "I" am feeling. What "I" need. What "I" want to do. The key is to remind them they are not there to serve themselves. Think of the mission the Savior was given. Possibly your reviewing with your homesick missionary the Savior's mission and his response will help.

In Moses 4:1–4 is recorded the account of the choosing of Christ as the Savior and Lucifer's subsequent rebellion. The Savior said: "Father, thy will be done, and the glory be thine forever" (Moses 4:2). That all sounds really easy until we read what the resurrected Christ told the Nephites the "will of the Father" really was. In 3 Nephi 27:13-14 the Savior says: "Behold I have given unto you my gospel, and this is the gospel which I have given unto you—that I came into the world to do the will of my Father *because my Father sent me.* And my Father sent me that I *might be lifted up upon the cross* . . . (3 Nephi 27:13-14; emphasis added). You mean Christ came specifically to suffer? Yes, and He came not because he particularly wanted to but because "my Father sent me."

I think it helps the missionaries to realize that missions are not all fun and games. A mission is not an endless string of spiritual experiences. Missions are difficult, challenging, sometimes distasteful, and occasionally downright miserable. But those times "came to pass." They did not "come to stay." These feelings will pass, and when they do, your missionary's ability to empathize with those who are suffering will increase dramatically.

My experience leads me to conclude that a heartfelt expression of understanding and encouragement may be all that is necessary to keep things in proper eternal perspective. If you take a penny and hold it within a half an inch of your right eye and close your left eye, what can you see? Only the penny. Does that mean that the penny is larger than the entire world that it is blocking from your vision? Of course not. The problem is that the penny is out of perspective. Tape the penny on a wall and stand back ten feet and one can see how small and insignificant the penny really is. Stand back a hundred feet and you cannot see the penny. Stand back a mile and you cannot see the wall! The time away from home, the newness of the surroundings, the difficulty of the language, the strangeness of the daily routine all are like pebbles on a path—so annoying while walking on the path but invisible from a plane flying a thousand feet about the path.

If you find your missionary is still struggling, try the "zoom out" technique. On most word processing programs or graphic programs on a computer, there is a feature which allows the user to "zoom out" and see the letter or graphics in a broader perspective. That same technique is valuable in helping missionaries realize what is happening to them. I firmly believe when we view our missionary experience or our life's experience from the vantage point of eternity, we will see that each of these painful experiences will have purpose and direction. We need to exercise enough faith to allow the Lord to mold us into a vessel he can use later in life.

An example may illustrate my point. One activity concocted in the ovens of outer darkness is thinning sugar beets. Some of you may have had similar experiences. The hoe used to thin the sugar beets had a handle about 12 to 18 inches long. This requires the person thinning the beets to bend over to reach the extra little beets which need to be pulled out to allow the others room to grow. The sun is always directly overhead and burning hot. The rows seem to be fifty miles long although they are generally only two blocks long.

One particularly hot day I must have projected the image of total discouragement. As I straightened up I thought my back would snap in two. The old farmer noticed my plight. He came to where I was and handed me a bottle of sun-heated water to quench my thirst. He was not a man of many words. He simply said, "Look how far you've come!" As I turned to look at the end of the row, I was amazed the distance I had covered. With renewed determination I tackled the task again. Admittedly, I had to "look how far I'd come" several times before I reached the end of the row.

Sometimes we need to do that with life. When missionaries would become discouraged and homesick, I would often invite them to "zoom out and look how far you've come." Not just the few days they had been in the field, not just the few years they have been here on earth preparing to serve, but look from an eternal perspective. I used to tease with the missionaries when they talked about how long they had left to serve. You will recall that in Abraham 3:4 it says that one day on Kolob (or with God) is equivalent to 1,000 years on earth. If you break that down a little, a normal year-and-a-half mission for sisters is 2 minutes and 9 seconds and a two-year mission for elders is equal to 2 minutes and 52 seconds in God's time! Every year we live in mortality is only 1 minute and 26 seconds long in God's time. Can't we be faithful for under 3 minutes of God's time in exchange for 100 times the blessings in temporal and spiritual affairs and the promise of eternal life in the world to come? Evaluate Mark 10:28–30 and see if those are not just a part of the promises made to faithful missionaries.

As you read through the Scriptures, especially the Doctrine and Covenants, you will be amazed at the promises the Lord has made to those who faithfully serve. It would require a large volume to record all the Lord has said about his missionaries. Set a reading schedule where you (at home) and your missionary (in the field) read a few sections each day looking for the promises. Then write back and forth about the promises you discover. Before either of you finish the Doctrine and Covenants, your missionary will want to stay—and you may even want to quit your job and go on a mission yourself! If you think I am jesting—take the challenge.

Wise parents are sensitive to certain times of the year when being separated from the family is especially difficult. The time between Thanksgiving and New Year's is particularly challenging for many missionaries. There may be other times (birthdays, family vacations, reunions) that naturally generate feelings of loneliness and separation. Redouble your efforts to keep your missionary focused on the mission.

In the very rare event nothing seems to work, in consultation with the bishop and stake president, contact the mission president. My experience was that we would pull onboard everybody we thought might help change the mind of those determined to go home. Sometimes a close friend, a quorum advisor, a Scout leader, a seminary or institute teacher, a patriarch, a grandfather, or favorite uncle could have a more moving effect than parents or mission presidents. Almost always missionaries with this type of support decided to stay and see it through.

If they are determined to come home in spite of all your efforts, accept their decision and welcome them back with open arms. They will suffer enough self-induced guilt without anyone saying anything. You will have to work harder than you ever have in your life to help them feel comfortable at church, in the family, and with their friends who successfully complete their missions. Homesickness can cloud the judgment and vision of young people to where they fail to consider the long-range effects of their decision.

Occasionally young people come home, get their head cleared, and are reassigned to another mission. If at all possible, encourage them to complete their mission. Work through your stake president to determine whether or when or if they should try again. A second failure could only compound the problems of coming home. Very often it is not desirable for them to return to the first mission.

They may feel they are letting the Lord down if they go somewhere else. They need to know the difference between a "call" and an "assignment." The "call" is to be a missionary. The "assignment" can change as frequently as being transferred in the mission field. Because both the call and the assignment come in the same letter, the missionary may not realize the difference. This is where you, as parents, must take some time explaining how things work. If you do not understand, contact a former mission president or someone on the missionary committee of the Church. It would not be unusual for a bishop or stake president not to understand the difference unless they have specifically been faced with that question.

Working closely with priesthood leaders about whether to go for another mission will give you a lot of ideas on ways to help your missionary cope with the added trauma of coming home early. The scope of this book does not permit us to investigate all the ramifications and considerations of someone who comes home early. Thankfully, the vast majority of those called end up serving their entire time. This brief period of homesickness is something we look back at and laugh, but it certainly is no laughing matter while those we love go through it.

Check with others, both parents and returned missionaries, to see how they dealt with the problem. I hope that some of the suggestions in this chapter will decrease the time and the intensity of such an experience for your missionary, if that happens to be part of his or her challenge.

Is it likely that homesickness will return after the initial bout? It very well could. The death of a family member (especially a close grandparent) can rekindle the desire to come home early. Be very sensitive about a "Dear John" or a "Dear Jane." They can be very difficult on missionaries, no matter how long they have served. Since only about 10 percent of those special someones wait, it is fairly safe to assume a missionary will be receiving that dreaded letter. Sometimes the marriage of a brother or sister causes homesickness to recur. An extremely challenging companion, a difficult area, a change of mission president, or any of a number of like occurrences may trigger another bout with home-sickness. Be sensitive to what your missionary is writing and you'll be able to help your child through tough times whenever they occur during the mission.

12

HELPING YOUR MISSIONARY
BE OBEDIENT

BEING ON A MISSION IS EXCITING, busy, and demanding. When those experiences are shared with parents, your lives are greatly enriched and the blessings of the mission are not confined strictly to the missionary. One reason the "white Bible" (Missionary Handbook) makes it mandatory for the missionary to write home is so you can enjoy and benefit from those experiences you are helping to support either financially, emotionally, or both.

You may be prone to excuse your son or daughter if he or she misses writing for a week or two because of being too involved in the work. Do not make that mistake. Remember the Lord never did say: "I the Lord am bound if ye do 80 percent of what I say . . . ." He did say: "I, the Lord am bound if ye do what I say, but if ye do not what I say, ye have no promise" (D&C 82:10). Your missionary cannot enjoy the fullness of the Spirit unless he or she is 100 percent obedient. Part of obedience is writing home every week without failure.

A helpful suggestion is for parents to send twice as much journal paper with your missionary as will be needed. The record missionaries write in their personal journal will contain elements they may not feel inclined to share with you at the time. If you have them send their weekly letters to you on the same kind of journal paper as their personal journal, it is easy to have a matching journal binder to catalog their letters. For years to come they will have their journal and their letters home to refer to as they recall the valuable lessons learned in the mission field.

What do you do if they don't write? Gently but firmly write them a letter explaining the absolute necessity of their writing if they are to be counted among the valiant missionaries. Help them put priorities on their P-day time. The white handbook spells out that before any other activities on P-day the missionaries are to write to the mission president (president's letter) and to their parents. If your son or daughter happens to get with a companion who does not see the value of keeping the rules, it is very easy for your missionary to follow suit. If you let your missionary know from before he or she enters the MTC what you expect, the chances are much better your missionary will follow through.

If your son or daughter is now serving and has fallen into the bad habit of not writing weekly, it may require some straight talk from you and maybe even a little encouragement from the mission president to correct the problem. On a number of occasions, I would get calls from parents who would say something like "Is my son still serving in your mission?" I would assure them he was and would inquire why they asked. The answer was always the same: "Well, it has been over a month since we've heard from him." I would assure them their missionary was all right and they would be hearing from the missionary directly. As I hung up the phone, I would dial the missionary. I would generally ask how his broken arm was mending. When he assured me he didn't have a broken arm, I would jokingly tell him he would have if his parents didn't get a letter as fast as the postal service could deliver it. The missionary was generally good natured about it and made up some of the most creative excuses for not writing. I would laugh with the missionary and then tell him death was the only acceptable excuse for not writing. With a good swift verbal kick, he would agree to write. I would then extract a promise this would not happen again. At that point I would reteach the principle of obedience. Generally one phone call was enough to help the missionary remember to write home weekly for the rest of his mission.

As a mission president, did I mind those calls from parents? On the contrary, I welcomed them. Without that kind of cooperative effort, it would be next to impossible to know which missionaries were regularly writing home. The far more serious problem for the mission and the mission president is when missionaries lose the spirit because of disobedience. When the Spirit leaves, the work does not get done, problems between companionships arise, disobedience becomes easier to rationalize, and the cycle continues endlessly downward until someone breaks it.

A form of disobedience innocently fostered by parents is the telephone calling card. You may feel you are making sure your missionary does not get caught in a compromising situation without the means of getting help. Over ninety-nine out of every hundred situations can be remedied by the ingenuity of the missionaries and the intervention of the Lord. Seldom, if ever, does the Lord require the parents to break a mission rule in order to save a missionary. In fact, I never saw or heard of such an example in the three years I served as mission president.

It is difficult to learn to rely solely upon Heavenly Father. It is much easier for a missionary to call home and get some advice from Mom and Dad. The results of those "unauthorized calls" is the loss of the Spirit and the postponing of the time when the missionary learns to rely on the ever-present, all powerful Heavenly Father. Do not interfere with the Lord's educational process.

Missionaries cannot afford to have calling cards. In saying that, I have no reference to the financial capability of either the missionary or the parents. Spiritually, missionaries are retarding their progress and maturity to the point where no informed parent would contribute to such a damning act.

Missions policies about calling home are well known to the missionaries. If your missionary hesitates informing you about the rule, write or call the mission president. As with so many other areas, just because the missionary does not see the value behind the rule does not mean there is not sound reasoning for it. Once the mission president informs you as parents about the reasons behind the rule, you will be much more likely to support the rule than the disobedience of your son or daughter.

You might ask about the occasional emergency. Wouldn't it be a lot more efficient if you could just call directly? No. Again drawing upon the experience of being with and shepherding over 600 missionaries, I know it is far better for you to contact the mission president when an emergency arises. I can't envision a mission president who would want to keep you from communicating with your son or daughter. But there are several compelling reasons to communicate with the mission president first.

First, it allows the mission president to counsel with you on the most appropriate time to inform your missionary. If a relative of the missionary has died, a few more hours without the missionary knowing won't change anything.

Second, it allows the mission president time to travel to the missionary, if you both deem it necessary. I have held massive young men in my arms and comforted them as they expressed their grief at receiving the news a father or mother had died or a brother or sister had been killed or injured in an accident. It may be decided between you and the mission president that it would be best for the president to break the news. After a time of counsel and comforting, the missionary (with the president sitting there for additional support) can call and discuss with the parents how to proceed.

A third reason for going through the mission president is it gives the president an opportunity to make arrangements to "cover" for the missionary in the event it seems expedient for him or her to return home. Along those same lines, it gives the president an opportunity to inform and instruct companions and others on how to help your missionary. A mission president want to do what is best for your son or daughter. It is next to impossible if he is unaware of your involvement with the missionary.

The examples of what happens when this procedure is not followed are long and many. Just one short story will suffice. I was at home early one morning before the day started and received a panic call from an elder who was stationed about 120 miles away. From the tone of his voice I could tell he was beside himself, not knowing what to do. After calming him a little so he could talk coherently, he explained that he feared for his companion, who had been talking suicide most of the night. I gave him some directions on how to act and left immediately to give some assistance. Thankfully the Highway Patrol cooperated and within a short time I was there with the troubled elder. After many hours, multiple prayers, several walks around the block, reading counsel and advice from the Scriptures, and letting him vent his frustrations, I was able to return home. He promised not to try anything irrational and to call if the pressure got too great.

I arrived home late that night physically and emotionally drained. As I prepared for bed the phone rang. The voice on the other end was a man's voice; he explained he was the troubled elder's father. He said he thought he had better inform me that he and his wife were getting a divorce and hoped the announcement would not interfere with his son's mission. He assured me that he had talked to his son the day before and that everything was all right. I must admit fatigue had loosened the chords of restraint on my tongue. I told him I had just spent the last eight hours trying to talk his son out of committing suicide. What the father could not see over the telephone, that I could see in person, was the total devastation the young man was going through. The father seemed surprised at his son's reaction. I was overtly irritated at his insensitivity. Over the final year of the elder's mission, I spent many days trying to help him recover from that one well-intentioned but unauthorized phone call.

Missions are designed by the Almighty to be tough. Testimonies are gained and direction cemented, which is essential if your missionary is to fulfill his or her divine foreordination. If phone cards are used to call friends, girl/boy friends, other missionaries, acquaintances within the mission, school buddies, or whoever, the learning process is greatly diluted. Please, don't contribute to their disobedience by providing them the means to disobey.

As your missionary writes home weekly, be alert to the content of the letters. If he or she talks of nothing but the scenery, the P-day activities, the goofing off that is going on in the apartment, put up a red flag. Missionaries who are really into the work will discuss investigators, spiritual experiences, lessons they are learning from the zone conferences or from life in general. That is not to imply they should never talk about scenery or recreational activities. Those too are part of a missionary's life. But they are only a small part if the missionary is doing his or her job.

You may need to teach your missionary how to write letters by the questions you ask. The average teenager can think of a thousand things he would rather do than write a lengthy letter. If you know what to look for, you can tell the very minute he/she catches the spirit of missionary work. Letters will become more serious and focused than before. If you never hear about any of the "work," make it a point to ask.

For a very nominal fee, you can obtain the white handbook from a Distribution Center. Remember that the only person in your son's or daughter's mission who has the right to amend what is in the white handbook is the mission president. If your missionary suggests that a certain rule has been set aside (for example, calling home whenever they please), challenge the suggestion. If the missionary persists, inform your missionary that you intend to call the mission president to verify the new rule. Usually that will bring a swift reversal.

In one of my missionary preparation classes at BYU a young woman said her missionary called almost every night after 10:30 p.m. He claimed it was with the mission president's approval. I suggested she have him read from the white handbook the pages that forbid calling girlfriends. He called again that night and steadfastly insisted that he was not breaking any rules. Not knowing what to do, the young lady asked my opinion. I said for her to tell her missionary that she was going to put him on hold while she got the mission president on a conference call so she could hear from the president's own lips that the calls were authorized. I predicted his reaction. He would fall all over himself to make sure she didn't call the president. Then I suggested that she inform him that she intended to marry an honorable, obedient returned missionary and that if he called again, she would cross him off her list of potential mates. The class gasped at the suggestion. Then I asked her, "If your friend is willing to cheat on the Lord, what makes you think he will be faithful to you in marriage?" The point was made and her report back was most gratifying to all of us. She said that after she followed my advice there was a long pause on the other end of the line. He thanked her for teaching him correct principles and vowed to a 100 percent obedient missionary from then on. He was true to his word.

Be sensitive to the plight of other missionaries who are serving with your son or daughter. When your missionary requests extra money, or receives an overabundance of "care packages," or receives any extra privilege, it puts undue stress on the companion whose parents are not able or willing to do the same. It is not that your missionary should go without—this is more a caution to be aware that a greater percentage of missionaries than you care to believe receive little or no support from home. Because of our "imposed sensitivity" as mission president, we would include a little something for our daughters' companions when we sent anything to them. It didn't hurt us, but from the overwhelming expressions of gratitude from their companions, we know it was worth every penny we spent on them.

Infrequently, missionaries request that items which are illegal in the mission field be sent from home. Tapes, CD's, magazine subscriptions and the like divert their attention and enable them to waste valuable proselyting time fussing over worldly things. The Lord's chastisement to David Whitmer shows His disapproval of worldly things on missions. "But your mind has been on things of the earth more than on the things of me, your Maker, and the ministry whereunto you have been called" (D&C 30:2). The result was that David was left to figure out on his own, without the Spirit, what he was doing wrong.

In the unlikely event your missionary writes about something in violation of the rules, caution him or her in your next letter that it is too expensive to have them out there disobedient. If you sense the work is not being seriously attended to, write or call the mission president with your concern. A couple of rather sobering statements have been made by Church leaders about the need for diligence by our missionaries. For your future use (if necessary), I am including them.

President Henry D. Moyle (Address to California Mission, June 2, 1962) stated:

I shall go to my grave saying that missionaries . . . never rise in their entire life above the stature they carve out for themselves in the mission field. I ask the missionaries all over the world to write that in their book, and then read the book ten years from now. If perchance, they have not risen in that first ten years after they come home from the mission field, above that status of mediocrity that they [may have] maintained in the mission field, [they should] get down on their knees, pray, and work a little harder and seek to overcome that tremendous handicap they placed upon themselves by their lack of application, lack of appreciation, and lack of dedication in the mission field.

Joseph Fielding Smith said in part:

They were to remember also that one important duty which they were to fulfill and that was to be sure and bear testimony in every instance. If they performed their labors sincerely, humbly and diligently bearing witness of the restoration then it would be more tolerable for the heathen in the day of judgment, than for that house which rejected the message. If no warning had been left, however, then the judgment would be pronounced against the servant who was expected to deliver it. . . . The elders who delivered the message were also to be judges in the day of judgment against those who rejected their testimony. Missionaries of the Church should realize this fact. They are sent to warn the world and when they faithfully do their duty they will stand as witnesses against those who reject them, but if they fail to perform their duty, then those unto whom the message should have been given, will stand up as accusers in their turn, and the unfaithful servants will be condemned. (*Church History and Modern Revelation* [Salt Lake City: Deseret News Press, 1946], 2:46–47)

Your missionary is sent to succeed. Without the help of the Lord, he or she cannot enjoy success like the faithful. Present-day missionaries have the distinct disadvantage of growing up in a world where emphasis on obedience has not been the primary focus. Sometimes it requires some pretty straight talk before they realize that a mission, although a great experience, comes with heavy responsibility. What a singular blessing to have parents and loved ones who are older and more focused who can constantly encourage the developing missionary to faithful diligence.

The pattern of strict obedience established in the mission field provides a rock-solid foundation upon which to build the rest of their mortal lives. Marriages performed in the temples will develop into eternal marriages if that same strict obedience to all the rules is applied as it was in the mission field. Less than obedient performance sets a pattern that is lethally dangerous to eternal marriages. Even if they are too young to envision the long-range effects of disobedience, you must do all you can to help them avoid the mistakes so common to missionaries. This is not "their mission." They are on the "Lord's mission" and they are not entitled to cheat him.

What a difference it would make if we could instill in all missionaries (male or female) the true meaning of their calling. This is the only time I wish we could call "Sisters," "Elders." President Harold B. Lee taught: "The term 'elder,' which is applied to all holders of the Melchizedek Priesthood, means a defender of the faith.

That is our prime responsibility and calling. Every holder of the Melchizedek Priesthood is to be a defender of the faith" (Conference Report, April 1970, p. 54). We must teach our missionaries to defend the faith not only by their words and arguments but also by their daily actions. Then the missionary work of the Church will accelerate at an unprecedented rate.

13

······

LEADERSHIP AND YOUR MISSIONARY

YOU HAVE ALWAYS KNOWN your son was to become the next Ammon of the latter days. As I daily interface with the next generation on missionaries, I am also constrained to admit if I had been required to compete with them for leadership positions I probably would have come home a junior companion. This is a noble and great generation of young people.

One of the natural consequences of growing up in a very competitive world is our tendency to judge our success on the positions we hold or the honors we receive. Perhaps if you put yourself into the shoes of the mission president, you will see how difficult it is to give every deserving young man a chance to lead. Many missions have of about 200 missionaries. Usually at least 75 percent of them are young elders. In a mission with 150 elders there are usually 10 to 15 zones. Each zone has two or three districts. The president can choose two elders to work with him as assistants to the president. If each zone has one zone leader and each district has one district leader, including the assistants, no more than 50 to 60 elders can serve in leadership positions at any given time.

Although it is desirable to give as many as possible a chance to develop their leadership skills, it is almost impossible to include everyone. We tried to spread leadership opportunities around by calling and releasing at regular intervals. The missionaries reacted well to the plan to include everyone. Sometimes it was the parents who had difficulty understanding.

A colleague told me the following experience. He was in the office working as assistant to the president. One P-day he was sitting with the mission secretary, who was an excellent missionary and almost indispensable to the successful operation of the mission. As they opened their letters for the week, the secretary started to cry. My friend asked if something was wrong. The secretary responded by pushing the letter he was reading towards my friend. The letter read in part: "Dear Son, What is the matter with you? You have been out eleven months and haven't even been called as a district leader? Why, your brother was a zone leader when he had been out only ten months . . . "

As a mission president, it is difficult to imagine how a parent could be so insensitive. A little reflection will reveal that during his entire three-year ministry Christ never once held a position! As far as his followers were concerned, he was one thing—a trainer. In the estimation of most mission presidents, a trainer is the most coveted and highest office any elder or sister can be called to fill. Think about it. If a missionary is a district or zone leader or even an assistant to the president and he completes his mission, the position is filled the very same day. Everything goes on without interruption. But a trainer has the ability to influence the way the mission goes for the next two years and probably much longer!

As we struggled to implement our rotational leadership style, the missionaries adjusted well. One day

I received a phone call from a parent suggesting his son was devastated at having been "demoted." I was genuinely concerned that no elder get that impression since our objective was to build and edify. I immediately drove to where the missionary was serving. In an intense interview he reassured me he felt fine about being released. When he questioned my concern, I told him about the phone call. He seemed to understand that position meant a great deal to his father and confessed he should have warned me about the possibility of such a phone call. I thought it very interesting the son could adjust without embarrassment but the father could not.

Many young men will serve in leadership positions. The added burden of caring for others does not lessen their responsibility in their own areas. At times it seems unfair to put these young men under such pressure. We are the ones who cower under the weight of their calling, not them. Unless they are prepared and warned, they may be surprised when they experience an increase in the temptations the adversary puts in their way. As you communicate with them, encourage them to keep their guard up and be constantly aware of what is going on around them.

Those missionaries whose parents wrote positive, upbeat letters of encouragement seemed to hold up better under the pressure of leadership than those whose parents either did not write or were constantly negative and complaining when they did write. Earth life is meant to be a test, a tough test at that. It is so easy to get trials out of focus and start complaining about our lot in life. It is infinitely more desirable to receive solid counsel on how to cope with a situation than a letter telling us how unfair life is and adding fire to our self-initiated pity party.

If a situation is really serious and needs immediate attention, contact the mission president through your bishop or stake president. Before you do, however, stop and think how often anyone smoothed the way for you during the trials of your growing up years. Most of you will admit you had to tough it out and you turned out better for it. Don't be a rescuer. Those same difficult tests which developed your character will also help steel your son or daughter for the difficult days ahead.

Sometimes your missionary may complain to you about situations in the apartment or between certain missionaries. If you feel something ought to be done, encourage them to talk it over with their apartment mates. If that does not remedy the problem, suggest they ask for advice from the mission president. They may be reluctant to talk because they are afraid of being labeled a "nark." However, unless they learn to go through the proper line of authority to solve the problem, the potential character-developing benefit will be lost.

Late one night I received a phone call from an anxious mother. Her son had called her to complain about something he did not like. The irony was I had spent an hour in an interview with him earlier in the day. During the interview he said everything was going fine. Between us we devised a plan to help him learn. She was to write back encouraging him to contact me. She was to teach the principles we have been discussing in this chapter. We decided it would be better not to mention our phone conversation. She agreed to keep me informed if conditions continued to deteriorate. A week later the young elder called and requested a follow-up interview. As we met, without mentioning the telephone call to his mother, he expressed his concerns and we devised a plan of attack. He also was instructed to keep me informed of the developments. Over the next month he reported regularly in his weekly "president's letter." The problems were solved, the friendships strengthened, and the follow-up note from his mother reassured me we had helped this young man learn a valuable lesson about solving problems through the proper channels.

Not all problems work out so smoothly. Occasionally it is necessary to maintain a sustained line of communication through your bishop or stake president to the mission president. Because the mission president is so closely involved in the running of the mission, he may have some very strong feelings about what ought to be done. Because the missionary belongs to you, you may have equally strong feelings about what is the correct course to pursue. A caring bishop or stake president can present your position without giving in to the temptation to verbally attack the mission president. Unless the mission president suggests otherwise, it is generally desirable to go through your leaders before contacting him directly.

If your son writes home expressing his disappointment at not being chosen as a leader, remind him that the day will come when he will long to be "just a senior companion." Leadership complicates the missionary's life and requires dividing his attention between proselyting and leading. Sometimes both areas suffer as he learns that "leadership is not all it is cracked up to be." A reinforcement and reassurance from you that it is "how" you serve rather than "where" you serve that makes the difference can make all the difference to the missionary. These young men really do want to please their parents. If we base our approval on the positions they hold, we are fostering a false criteria for serving a successful mission.

As a leader, your son will be required to conduct meetings, give talks, and interview missionaries and potential converts. He will attend administrative meetings, solve problems between missionaries, act as a liaison between missionaries and ward leaders, and become a master record keeper. He will inspect apartments, give reports to the mission leadership, receive and pass on instructions from the mission president to his district or zone, and constantly monitor their "stats." (statistical record of their activities). In addition he will be expected to set an example of what an effective missionary is like. Is it any wonder the weight of leadership almost cries out to us for some help? Frequently our Area Presidency would tell us "a well-served, two year mission is equivalent to fifty years of normal church service." Allow your missionaries to experience the "highs" and "lows" of leadership. Be thrilled with them and for them as they grow in ways you have always prayed they would grow. Let the Lord determine how quickly they have some of the soul-stretching experiences that are built into the very fiber of leadership in the mission field. Since they will have an adequate number of challenges in their leadership positions, be very sensitive that you do not become part of their problem!

It may be frightening for you to contemplate the caliber of leader in the future who would require the magnitude of problems your son is facing as a preparation. It seems obvious that the Lord does not do anything frivolously or without purpose. Surely all of the lessons learned from the experiences missionaries are going through will be used to the fullest as they face the future. Be a supportive voice on the sidelines cheering them on with encouraging words as they face the challenges devised by a loving, caring Divine Father.

14

GETTING THE MOST I POSSIBLY CAN

WHAT A THRILL IT WOULD BE if all parents could be in the mission field at the airport to witness their arriving missionaries. These missionaries are a unique combination of fear, nervous energy, enthusiasm, fatigue, restlessness, and desire. To listen to them express their dreams for a mission, one would be tempted to believe the Millennium had arrived and this was the first compliment of missionaries to be prepared by a celestial faculty at the MTC. It would be equally as desirable if parents could see how difficult serving to the end with all their "heart, might, mind, and strength" really is.

The only mile race I ever ran was as a freshman in high school. The track coach enlisted me because no one else was around. He assured me I didn't have to run very fast, just stay ahead of the guy right behind me. I don't remember ever training for the event and certainly was not properly conditioned for the ordeal. But with all the boyish enthusiasm of youth, I started the race. The first of the four laps wasn't bad. We all looked as if we were about equal in our skill level. The second lap was more difficult. Some dropped out because of pain in their sides or cramping leg muscles. I plodded along staying "just in front of the guy right behind me." Before the third lap was half over, I could tell I was in trouble. My lungs were burning, my muscles cramping, and my spirits drooping. It was then I became aware of the coach, other team members, and members of the student body shouting encouragement as I hobbled along. Just knowing they were there gave me added strength. As the fourth and final lap began, I and "the guy right behind me" were considerably ahead of the rest of the pack. He was determined to win the race and I was equally as determined to stay just ahead of him. As we rounded the final curve and started down the straightaway towards the finish line, the muscles in my legs seized up and I thought I could go no further. I was about ready to drop out when I again became aware of the cheering section. They lined the track on both sides. They were screaming, cheering, urging, and running along pacing me. How could I quit? With the last ounce of energy at my command, I sprinted (it couldn't have been faster than a slow walk!) across the finish line. I'd won! I collapsed into the arms of the coach whose congratulatory strikes on my back probably started my heart going again after a moment of full cardiac arrest. He literally dragged me off the track and laid me on the grass. My hour of glory had come. I was hailed as the greatest mile runner on the freshman team—I was the only one!

Why tell such a story? If you could see how difficult it is to keep going day after endless day as a missionary, you would know how vital the "cheering section" is at home. To a missionary who just arrived in the field, eighteen months or two years seems like an eternity. To a bone-tired missionary who has a year or nine months left, the last lap seems impossible. As parents at home, you may be aware that most of their friends stop writing regularly after a few months. With your encouragement, the Young Women's leaders can be persuaded to have the girls write occasionally. Relief Society sisters (especially those who have had sons or daughters serve before) are more than willing to write. Bishoprics can send a monthly letter including the ward newsletter. The elders and high priests can write. Some of the highlights of our missionaries' lives were when they received letters written by Primary children.

A lukewarm effort does not result in the superior blessings promised to the faithful missionary. Note the promise made by the Lord in Doctrine and Covenants 84:79-80:

"Behold, I send you out to prove the world, and the laborer is worthy of his hire.

And any man that shall go and preach this gospel of the kingdom, and *fail not to continue faithful in all things,* shall not be weary in mind, neither darkened, neither in body, limb, nor joint; and a hair of his head shall not fall to the ground unnoticed. And they shall not go hungry, neither athirst." (emphasis added)

Weekly encouragement from you in the form of letters, quotes, stories, articles from Church magazines, and selected scriptures can be a great motivating factor.

Most of the missionaries we supervised were more than anxious to please their parents. Sure, the ideal is to have them work because of their love of the Lord and his gospel, but until they mature to that point, it doesn't hurt to have an ulterior righteous motive for service.

At times the vision of youth about what can be done is somewhat lacking. You may be able to identify with that statement when you consider what many young people consider a "hard day's work" compared with what you did as a child. Although our own children are hard workers, they are more prone to take a "breather" long before my wife and I are accustomed to stopping. We get razzed occasionally with the "We know! You walked four miles to school each day in two feet of snow and it was uphill both ways!" routine. But when they try to match our pace for very long, their stamina is lacking. The greatness of the Church and your personal lives were not built on frequent breaks and rest periods. If we can urge missionaries to give the extra effort and go the extra mile, they will find (as you have) most of the rewards are hidden in the second mile. Once they have tasted the sweetness of the rewards for 100 percent service, they will motivate themselves. Until they see the actual fruits of their labors, they may be reluctant to pay such a high price.

Occasionally missionaries would share with me letters from home. Upbeat, newsy letters were greatly appreciated. Complaining, negative letters only added to the already difficult task of keeping their spirits up. Artificially camouflaged letters claiming everything was "OK" when real problems existed were also not helpful. The last two statements may have sounded somewhat contradictory—and therefore a word of explanation is in order. When petty, nonthreatening, normal fluctuations of life happen, there is little or no benefit in burdening your missionary with those things over which he or she has no control and no stewardship. Almost everyone goes through minor bouts with discouragement and depression. Rumors about possible layoff's at work are only that—rumors! Wait for the "pink slip" before dropping the bombshell. Also, unless specific encouragement from the missionary to a younger brother or sister could really help a problem situation, it would be less stress producing to keep those kinds of problems on the quiet side.

However, when a missionary knows a favorite grandfather is dying of cancer, regular updates can actually reduce worry. These young people are taught to "read between the lines" with their investigators. They are encouraged to be sensitive to the unspoken message. Therefore, when you write there is serious friction that could result in the breakup of the family, it is helpful to give a general warning but not a blow-by-blow account. The fine line between trivial and serious is not clearly defined. I have been a firsthand witness of the devastating effects of keeping important, life-altering situations from a missionary until the event is past. I have also been a more frequent party to family matters unwisely shared which divert attention from the missionary's work.

Perhaps drawing your attention to the problem is sufficient to encourage you to prayerfully consider the possible impact of the information you anticipate sharing. Certainly the intent is not to tell you what you can or cannot write, but since your implied purpose for "lending" your missionary to the Lord is to have him or her make a substantive contribution to the progress of the kingdom of God, it would be counterproductive to undermine your own efforts.

Another area where balance is sometimes lacking is the proper mixture of humor and seriousness. As a young missionary, I was reading the Doctrine and Covenants for the first time when I came upon the admonition of the Lord: "Therefore, cease from *all your light speeches,* from *all laughter,* from all your lustful desires, from all your pride and *light-mindedness*, and from all your wicked doings" (D&C 88:121; emphasis added). Being a innately cheery person, yet wanting to be totally obedient, I immediately wiped the smile off my face. For three or four days I walked around looking very serious, but also noticing an unmistakable diminution of the Spirit. Several missionaries asked if anything was wrong. I responded that everything was all right, that I was just trying to obey the commandments. My rather morose state became so noticeable a zone leader asked me to explain what I was doing that caused the Spirit to withdraw. I opened to the previously quoted verse and read it to him. He began to laugh and proceeded to teach me a powerful lesson. You can make the Scriptures say anything you want if you take things out of context and in isolation from the rest of the gospel or even the setting in which they were given. He referred me to verse 117, which sets the stage: "Therefore, verily I say unto you, my friends, call your *solemn assembly*, as I have commanded you" (emphasis added). It seemed so obvious to me then. During a solemn assembly there is not a place for any laughter at all! I had completely ignored the Lord's counsel just fifty-two verses earlier where He said: "Remember the great and last promise which I had made unto you; cast away your idle thoughts and your *excess of laughter* far from you" (D&C 88:69; emphasis added). I had also failed to register the Lord's Sabbath counsel: "And inasmuch as ye do these things with thanksgiving, with cheerful hearts and countenances, *not with much laughter*, for this is sin, but with a glad heart and a cheerful countenance . . ." (D&C 59:15; emphasis added). Immediately I put a smile back on my face and miraculously the Spirit returned.

I share this experience to alert you to a problem is not uncommon among missionaries who are trying to "live perfect lives." The problem is one of overcompensation. With a nonautomatic focusing camera, the photographer must manually focus the lens to the correct setting for maximum clarity for the intended object. If the camera is grossly out of focus, it is not unusual to make several major focal adjustments. Often the object becomes blurry as we overcorrect. Fine-tuning is required to achieve the desired results. Missionaries who need some major adjustments in their attitude and behavior (which we almost all do!) often overcompensate, going to the extreme. Wise, sensitive parents (sensing the problem through their missionaries letters) can give wise counsel to help them fine-tune.

If they had not been so sincere, it might have been humorous to watch missionaries go from too casual to too strict overnight. They may even view attempts by the mission president to get them to soften their approach a little as a lack of understanding or a halfhearted commitment to righteousness on his part. A second and third voice from home reinforcing the need to be patient and understanding of others as they continue to develop the attributes of righteousness is so helpful and welcome.

The overzealousness of newly converted missionaries to perfect their righteousness reminds me of the story told about a first-grade teacher who wanted to include her eager new students in formulating the rules for classroom discipline. She asked: "Children, what punishment shall we have for the student who breaks our classroom rules?" To her astonishment the almost unanimous voice of the class was "Kill them!" Hardly an acceptable punishment for breaking a minor classroom rule.

On more occasions than one would believe, I received calls from missionaries wanting me to "call Salt Lake and have them release Bishop So-and-So for his total lack of support of the missionary effort!" Those in church callings from stake president, bishop, ward mission leader, stake mission president, to Relief Society president have come under the condemning scrutiny of "overfocused" missionaries. Usually those missionaries would back way off when I asked whether they would be on a mission now if the same standard of judgment they were using against the Church leader in question had been used against them before their mission. The stark contrast helped them see the necessity of using a softer approach.

Too often these criticisms are voiced to you parents rather than to the mission president. I know, from the number of phone calls and letters I received from parents voicing their concerns about the Church leaders. I used to joke with the parents that if they wouldn't believe everything they heard about me, I would refrain from making a judgment against them based on what I had heard about them. Seldom do young missionaries have enough information to make summary decisions about the "rightness" or "wrongness" of a priesthood leader's decision.

The additional, but unnecessary stress accompanying decision-making outside our own stewardship can be and often is debilitating. If wise parents can help their missionary focus on matters over which he or she has stewardship and control, much of the wasted energy and concern can be eliminated. Vital but limited energy can be directed into more productive areas. The adversary never rests in his attempts to detract our attention into nonproductive areas. Wisdom gained by parents after years of experience (some gained in the school of hard knocks!) can bless the lives of young enthusiastic missionaries. By being supportive in the Lord's way, you can help them get the most they can out of their short missionary service.

If we are unsuccessful at getting missionaries to magnify their own calling and to let others magnify theirs, we run the risk of seeing our precious returned missionaries fall into the ranks of the apostates who seem more than willing to direct the leaders of the Church in how to magnify their callings. Some misdirected young people even want to direct the Lord on the revelations he gives and the way he directs his kingdom. One wonders if their course in life would have been different had they learned early on to worry more about magnifying their own office and less about trying to be the master controller of everyone else's office.

It is amusing to listen to, but annoying to go through, the readjustment period when recently returned missionaries try to "fix" all the broken parts in their family. It generally is not until they are married and have children that those missionaries realize how out of place they were in attempting to magnify Dad's and Mom's roles. Ignoring their well-intentioned but misdirected efforts only compounds their problems later in life. At the first sign of trouble, intercede and help your child put his or her role into proper perspective.

15

BEING PART OF YOUR MISSIONARY'S MISSION

There are obvious ways parents participate in their children's missions. Although the physical preparation period is expensive, it can be an extremely unifying experience. The emotion and Spirit associated with the farewell, the MTC, and the airport, all contribute positively to enjoyment of the fruits of a mission. But the real mission starts as the missionary arrives in his or her field of labor and begins doing what missionaries do. Having seen missionaries arrive on a monthly basis as well as sending our two oldest daughters on missions, we are keenly aware of the hopes and fears of parents concerning their welfare and safety. We shared with all parents the prayers pleading for a good trainer and a good area to begin their service. We realized how vital a good start was to the success of their missions and had to restrain ourselves from calling our girls' mission presidents to "suggest" what would be best for them. After all, who would be in a better position than a mission president father to give valuable advice? I'll tell you who—their own mission presidents! To the parents who have entrusted their most prized possessions (their sons and daughters) into the hands of the Lord, please allow the Lord to provide them with opportunities and experiences he knows they will need to prepare them for future responsibilities. Some well-meaning parents attempting to compensate for the human weaknesses of the mission president have tried to magnify the Lord's office. Remember the Lord's promise: "And ye cannot bear all things now; nevertheless, be of good cheer, for *I will lead you along . . .*" (D&C 78:18; emphasis added). I know from firsthand experience the Lord compensates for the limitations and weaknesses of the mission president. The Lord is not far from his missionaries. He speaks even more reassuring words calculated to put the hearts of worried parents at ease: "Behold, I send you out to reprove the world of all their unrighteous deeds, and to teach them of a judgment which is to come. And whoso receiveth you, there I will be also, for *I will go before your face. I will be on your right hand and on your left,* and my Spirit shall be in your hearts, and mine angels round about you, to bear you up" (D&C 84:88; emphasis added).

Realizing how wicked the world is could cause even the most stout-hearted parent considerable concern. Once again the Lord reassures us: "Verily, thus saith the Lord unto you—there is no weapon that is formed against you shall prosper; And if any man lift his voice against you he shall be confounded in mine own due time" (D&C 71:9–10). Easily an entire book could be written about the promises the Lord makes to his missionaries. Perhaps a final sampling of how closely he attends his ministers will suffice. He said: "And any man that shall go and preach this gospel of the kingdom, and fail not to continue faithful in all things, shall not be weary in mind, neither darkened, neither in body, limb, nor joint; and a *hair of his head* shall not fall to the ground unnoticed. And they shall not go hungry, neither athirst"

(D&C 84:80; emphasis added).

How are assignments made? How are companions chosen? How does the mission president determine how long to leave missionaries together and in a certain area? Those are all legitimate questions. Perhaps every president is slightly unique in his methodology. One thing all mission presidents will readily admit—the Lord has an unseen hand in the placement and movement of his servants. The event triggering a transfer is usually the arrival from the MTC of a new group of missionaries. That usually coincides with the release of (ideally) the same number of missionaries who have completed their missions. Unless there are extenuating circumstances, "midmonth" transfers are the exception rather than a norm.

In our mission we started working on transfers for the next month immediately following transfers. The mission is informed at least two to three months before your missionary arrives. The missionary department does a phenomenal job of keeping everybody straight. If you consider the logistical nightmare of trying to coordinate the calls, releases, MTC experiences (in multiple MTC's), the plane flights, passports, and visas of over 50,000 missionaries, you begin to see the complexity a worldwide church must deal with in just this one small area alone.

During the course of the month we would work and rework the proposed transfers several times. Because of the dynamic nature of missionary life, changes would be made as late as a couple of days before the actual transfer. Sometimes the necessity of changes was evident. A missionary completing his/her mission, sickness requiring doctor's attention or access to a car, need for a missionary to train a "greeny" from the MTC, serving in one area for an extended length of time, and so on. The factors involved in transfers were not all items we could put on a list. There were feelings and impressions which could not be denied. Sometimes there didn't seem to be a reason at all. We (in our mission—the president and his assistants) sometimes looked at each other somewhat bewildered as to why we were proposing a certain change. Over the months I learned not to ask so many questions. Some of the greatest miracles among missionaries resulted from placing missionaries together for reasons hidden from us.

One particular experience might satisfy as an illustration of my point. We were struggling to find appropriate companions for two sisters who had some particular needs. In an attempt to make sure all our areas were covered, we placed the two sisters together knowing they just would not work out as a companionship. Each time we met, the assistants would remind me we needed to find companions for these two sisters. I agreed but each time the session would end without either of them being moved. On the fifth and final go through the assistants became panicked. Something had to be done. I agreed. Each session of transfers is commenced with solemn and pleading prayer for Divine direction. We felt our prayers were not being answered. At the end of the fifth session the assistants emphatically said, "President, you know as well as we do these sisters cannot serve together. You must make a change!" I agreed with their analysis, but for some reason I couldn't change them. Even the warnings about the hours I would spend keeping them going and helping them become friends made no difference. I finally decided to leave them together and see what happened. To the amazement of us all, these two sisters hit it off and for the next five months were the best friends, the most productive companions, and a powerful, stabilizing influence in their district and zone. Only the Lord could have known what frail human beings refused to admit. Transfers were a lot easier for me after that experience.

At least once, probably several times during your missionary's service, he or she will have companions who are really difficult to live with. They may be assigned to areas where the work is really slow and progress is difficult. As they write home you may detect some complaining and discontent. Please be wise and write back encouraging them to learn every lesson they possibly can from the experience. To sympathize with them only makes conditions more impossible in their minds. Once they get on a "pity party" they fail to recognize the unparalleled opportunities for growth they are being given. Occasionally a distraught missionary would call demanding a transfer because he could not get along with his companion. I would often counter by explaining the lessons in compromise, negotiation, and patience he or she was learning and how valuable those skills would be in marriage. Not infrequently they would retort by saying they would never consider marrying someone like their companion. I would respond by saying, "You can choose your mate but you can't choose your children. You will probably have a child exactly like your companion. What will you do then, demand a transfer?" We would laugh and then discuss ways of coping with the situation. On rare occasions a transfer was the best solution—but only when confirmed by the Lord.

The problems associated with presiding over a mission are greatly multiplied when parents write or call demanding a transfer for their son or daughter. Those parents may never have stopped to consider that some other parents' son or daughter would have to be inconvenienced in order to spare their missionary the discomfort of serving with a developing missionary. What a complimentary testimonial to you and your missionary when the mission president assigns them to work with difficult companions. In many cases, your son or daughter could be the last-ditch attempt by the mission president to help that struggling elder or sister to complete an honorable mission. The difference between a missionary returning home early, a failure, a disappointment to himself, his family, the ward, the Church, and one who finishes honorably (albeit with less than perfect valor) cannot be calculated. Please think five or six times before demanding a transfer for your missionary. Calling General Authorities asking for their intercession in perceived problems is not teaching the valuable lesson of going through the proper channels. Your bishop or stake president can give you suggestions on how to proceed if you should not receive the help you feel you need from the mission president.

Only your missionary can determine the attitude with which he or she will serve a mission. Attitude makes all the difference in the world. Missionary after missionary reported in their weekly "president's letter" that a certain area was "dead" and needed to be closed. One overly enthusiastic companionship suggested we "knock the dust off our feet against the city." Finally we chose the most positive elder in the mission, gave him some preliminary counsel about what to expect, charged him to diligently try for a couple of months before we made such a drastic decision as closing an area. He went to work with his might. The first month, according to his own testimonial, was exactly what the other missionaries had reported. Undaunted, he continued to find clever ways of endearing himself to the members. Notes in the hymn books containing missionary thoughts or scriptures caused some raised eyebrows and smiles. Cards of appreciation were left at dinner appointments. Slowly hearts were softened. The second month resulted in more teaching appointments, more member support, and a better feeling in the ward. The third month brought five baptisms and by the fifth month there had been twenty-five baptisms and more projected for the future. All this from a "dead" area. The difference was the attitude of the missionaries, which in turn triggered the cooperation of the members.

If you sense a tone of pessimism in your missionary's letters, write back encouragement to attack the problem with optimism. Based on what has been prophesied about the future world into which your missionary will be projected, they will need all the optimism possible to be successful. Let them learn their first lessons in the mission field.

Is there ever a time to get involved with the mission president. Yes, but for sake of order, go through the proper channels—the bishop and stake president. Happy missionaries make happy mission presidents. No mission president is trying to make life miserable for the missionaries. His philosophy of how to discipline or get things done may differ from yours, but remember who was called to preside over the mission.

Some parents want to travel to the mission field and visit their missionary during their mission. The almost universal response of the missionaries we served with was they did not want the visit to interrupt their missionary work. It isn't just the hour or two you spend with them—it is the days before and the weeks following where focus on the work is more difficult which cause them to refuse visits from the people they love the very most. Some parents may interpret the refusal of their son or daughter as a lack of love. Just the opposite is true. They are trying to bring honor to your family by serving with "all their heart, might, mind, and strength." Contact the mission president for counsel and clearance before making plans for a visit.

A number of parents want to travel to the mission field and spend a couple of days with their missionary before returning home. Again, there are positive as well as negative factors involved in the visit. It certainly gives the parents a firsthand look at where the missionary has been serving. It is a wonderful opportunity to meet some of the people the missionary has served, loved, and baptized. It is a golden opportunity for parents to express their appreciation to special companions, mission leaders, and local members for their watchful care over the missionary. These are all just a few of the many positive aspects of family visits to the mission.

The downside of the visit is the disruption to the missionary work parents' presence causes. A missionary is not released in the mission field—the local stake president does the releasing. Therefore the missionary is still a full-time servant with a companion in a designated area. Arrangements must be made for his or her companion to "team up" with other missionaries, meaning only half the work can be done in the two areas since all three of the missionaries would have to serve together while the parents traveled with their missionary. As wonderful as it is to visit old areas, it is also disruptive to the efforts of those who are currently serving there. The problem is compounded if the missionary was especially loved by the people and those now serving there have not established the same relationship. The long-lasting effects of such a visit increases the difficulty of the current missionaries to win the hearts of the people.

Traveling from one area to another also poses a problem with the missionaries who have not completed their missions, as your missionary wants to "say good-bye" to old friends and companions. More "homesick-ness" is caused by farewells in the mission field between missionaries than almost any other factor. Obviously your missionary will talk about getting together at home, make plans for future trips, and a thousand other things young people dream about. When you leave, the dreams continue with the still-serving missionaries.

At times the local people feel obligated to feed the missionary and his family as a gesture of their love. Your missionary can verify how meager the family income is with so many of these faithful Saints. One large meal could consume the majority of a month's food budget. Being sensitive to their plight can help avoid many of the possible problems. Other families feel obliged to give gifts as tokens of their love and thankfulness. Again, too many families give beyond their capability, causing children to go hungry for the next month.

The overlying word is "caution" when visiting the mission. The mission president wants to meet you but he still has a mission to run. He is in the middle of the busiest part of the month—transfers. I felt so bad when I could see the excitement in the eyes of the missionaries who wanted me to meet and spend some time with their families only to be interrupted by a call to go to the airport to pick up the arriving missionaries. I am sure the families understood, but we still felt badly about not being able to spend more time together.

Finally, some mission presidents are well organized and able to communicate with families on a regular basis. Others are not computer literate and struggle with geographically large missions or challenging missionaries. From our experience, I wish we could have sent a monthly letter to each parent. Mailing to over 200 parents is expensive and time consuming. It is easy to say "let the secretary do it." The secretaries are pushed beyond their limits with work essential to the running of the mission. Be understanding when the letters from the president are infrequent and maybe in "form letter" style. I hope you agree if a choice has to be made between writing to parents and meeting the daily needs of the missionaries, that the top priority should be meeting the needs of the missionaries.

Mission presidents love and respect parents. Without your help their job would be impossible. By working together as a team, parents and mission presidents can reduce frustration, and soul-stretching learning experiences can be enjoyed by missionaries, parents, and mission leaders. Avoid at all costs becoming an adversary with the mission president. Share in every appropriate way the entire mission of your missionary. Surely missions bless everyone they touch.

16
....

SERVING VALIANTLY TO THE END

YOU WILL PROBABLY NOTICE as your missionary's mission
progresses he or she goes through different stages. We
have already discussed the first difficult stage—the
homesick stage. If you are not aware, you may think
homesickness is the most difficult stage. There is one
even more challenging—serving to the very end without
slacking off. Regrettably, missionaries for years have
developed and refined some ridiculous terms
designating different stages of their missions. The six-
month mark is referred to as "the bump." It is difficult to
generalize on the meaning since its meaning may vary
from mission to mission. In the missions where I have
some acquaintance, the "bump" means the missionary
no longer needs to rely solely upon the strength of
his/her trainer. Now they can bump their own mission
into gear and add some strength. The twelve-month
mark is termed "the hump." Almost universally it means
they have served as long as they have left. If the term
were really correct, it would be wonderful. However,
their reasoning begins to break down with the third
term designating the eighteen-month mark—"the slump."
At the very time when they are in the best position to
serve, either consciously or unconsciously, they are

tempted to put their spiritual transmission into "neutral" and coast to the end. At the end of their mission, the twenty-four-month mark, they tack on the label "dump." What a way to finish the "greatest two years of my life."

Somehow we need to overhaul their thinking lest the mere suggestion of "slump" and "dump" become self-fulfilling prophecies. We tried to encourage the missionaries to substitute "pump" for "slump." How much more appropriate to "kick it into overdrive" when they are the most effective. Just as a runners "kick" the last leg of the race, giving it all they've got, so the missionaries should redouble their efforts those final crucial months. Instead of ending the mission with a "dump" we encouraged them to adopt the term "jump." In very deed, if they have served with honor, their mission will become a springboard for the rest of their lives. The ring of the words "pump" and "jump" leave so much more positive a feeling than "slump" and "dump" that the missionary should be very willing to make the change.

Changing the terminology to "pump" and "jump" is only the first step. From our observation of over 600 missionaries, it requires a herculean effort to keep going strong those last few months. It is difficult to imagine parents would consciously sabotage the ending of their missionary's mission, but in reality many did. Having two daughters serve missions (one in France and one in Spain) while we were presiding over the California Fresno Mission, we have some firsthand knowledge of how difficult it is not to get "trunky" for them. I know how disappointed we were when we received the letter from France informing us our daughter had opted to stay until the February release rather than coming home for Christmas. In our heart of hearts we were bursting with pride at her desire to diligently serve to the very end. In our superficial heart, we could hardly contain our disappointment. We had been separated as a family for so long it just didn't seem fair. A few minutes of a self-serving pity party was sufficient to let us know how shortsighted we were. Our daughter could spend every Christmas for the rest of our lives with us if she so desired. This would be the last possible Christmas she would ever spend as a young, single sister missionary serving the Saints and investigators in France. We were more than a little ashamed of our "littleness of heart."

Our return letter to our daughter never hinted at our disappointment. We praised her for her decision and spoke anxiously about our "Christmas phone call." When she returned in February, our reunion was even that much sweeter. The children with us in California thought it was great to celebrate Christmas both in December and again in February.

We have heard of some very creative ways parents keep their missionary's attention focused on coming home. One mom counted the number of "garbage days" until her son's release date. It was humorous but not at all helpful. "Only twenty more garbage days to go." "Only nineteen more garbage days to go." The elder almost regretted getting the letter each week. Other parents wrote about the plans they were making for the welcome home scene at the airport. Every graphic detail was rehearsed again and again. How are the missionaries to serve "with ALL their heart, might, mind, and strength" when they are constantly teased into thinking about home?

It is difficult enough to keep them focused on "that which will be of most worth" (see D&C 15:6) when they are required to pause and fill out applications for college. Because the major universities are so competitive on their entrance requirements, the young people must start at least nine months before their proposed entrance date. We suggested they take one P-day and finish everything then refocus on the work. Most were more than happy to comply. Some decisions must be made and follow-through taken. It is really helpful if parents or brothers and sisters can handle the essential, but distracting, details. Our soon-to-graduate-from-high school daughter successfully filled out all three BYU applications although she wasn't always thrilled about doing it. She was a godsend for our two missionaries daughters.

Now having considered the two major problems from home (parents' writing homesick letters and school applications), let us us consider the problem of serving diligently to the end for the missionary. There is a term in physics which describes the problem quite well. It is *entropy*: The resistance to continued motion on a moving body. The tendency to move from a state of order to a state of chaos. The tendency of an energy body to run down. The missionary senses the same problem. How does a one keep going when one knows one will not be there to harvest the fruits, reap the rewards or see the baptism? Too many get to those crucial last months and adopt a defeatist attitude. "Why should I kill myself working when someone else will get credit for it?" A wise parent will sense when the subtle attitude change takes place. Encouragement from home, quotes from Church leaders, especially motivating scriptures, and examples from your own or other people's lives can make all the difference in the world.

We tried to think of the best example of all. As in every other imaginable positive example, the Savior wins. We would ask the missionaries to consider how they would be personally affected if the Savior had decided to just "kick back and goof off" his last week. To young women and men who have spent the last year-and-a-half or two years respectively studying the life of the Savior, the impact was overwhelming. They knew of the important doctrine He taught, the example of righteous indignation (cleansing the temple), the initiation of the Sacrament, the beginning of the Atonement in the Garden of Gethsemane, his marvelous example of Godly self-control during his mock trial, his completion of the Atonement on the cross, and his final victory over the grave to save us all. Consider the cost to everyone and everything that has ever or will ever live on this earth and to the earth itself. Consider the negative impact on countless other worlds if the Savior had "slumped' or 'dumped" just his last week.

How do you recognize the "slump"? Watch carefully in your missionary's letters. If he or she begins writing about home more than usual, it should raise a warning flag. Literally everything that is important will wait until that which is "most important" is complete. If the focus of their letters turns from talking about spiritual experiences, converts, discussions, doctrine and principles, to matters unrelated to a mission, your encouragement can help them refocus. If P-day activities seem more important than the gospel, Scriptures, and the Spirit, your missionary is succumbing to entropy—write straight, hard advice. Even if you cannot detect a dip in diligence or focus, it wouldn't hurt to increase your encouragement to diligence.

The following poem by Douglas Mallock applies well to missionary work:

BILL BROWN

Bill Brown made a million—Bill Brown—think of that!
A boy, you remember, as poor as a rat!
He hoed for the neighbors, did jobs by the day;
But Bill made a million, or near it, they say.
You can't understand it? Well, neither could I.
And then I remembered, and now I know why:
    The Bell might be ringing, the dinner horn blow,
    But *Bill always hoed to the end of the row.*

Bill worked for my father, you maybe recall;
He wasn't a wonder, no not that at all.
He couldn't out-hoe me, or cover more ground,
Or hoe any cleaner, or beat me around.
In fact, I was better in one way that I know—
One toot from the kitchen and home I would go.
    But *Bill always hoed to the end of the row.*

We used to get hungry out there in the corn;
When you talk about music, what equals a horn?—
A horn yellin' dinner—tomatoes and beans
And pork and potatoes and gravy and greens.
I ain't blaming no one for quitting on time.
To head home from the field is surely no crime.
But as for the million—well, this much I know—
    That *Bill always hoed to the end of the row.*

Perhaps you served a mission years ago. Can you
remember those last few days? If you are like me, you
can remember the ending as well as any other part of the
mission. If you ended off strong, you will always
remember the finish. Thankfully, the strong finish acts

like a wall to block from our memories the times we should have done better. We can look back and remember only the high points. In retrospect, I am quite sure I was not as diligent a missionary as I remember myself being. But I did end on a super high. Contrast the strong finish with missionaries who "slumps' and 'dumps." Going out on a low brings back feelings of disappointment and regret. As with most of Satan's temptations, we don't find out until too late how empty and hollow his promises really are. What a terrible "revelation" when less-than-diligent missionaries realize in the final hours of their time in the mission field that they have stolen from their own eternal piggy bank. Then it is too late. There just isn't a way to make up for missed opportunities, forfeited spiritual experiences, and unexperienced memories. In addition, the wall at the finish is so low they will easily remember the times they should have done better. What a shame to look back with regret on the "greatest two years of my life."

Perhaps you have noticed how subtly Satan works in your own life. He has a way of bringing "flashbacks" to mind at the most inappropriate time. He is even more cruel with missionaries. You will recall from our early discussion that there are 100,000 people out there in the world for every missionary. Satan is obviously very interested in disqualifying missionaries if he can, or at least neutralizing their effectiveness. As they hold up the light to bring others to Christ, it illuminates every chink in their armor. Even old transgressions they were sure had been taken care of come back to haunt them. If you (and they) know it is going to happen, it is much easier to deal with. If they are not expecting it, missionaries will likely be blindsided by these flashbacks in a confidence-shattering way. Like so many other ideas which have consciously been woven into this book, this tactic of Satan could make the nucleus of a good letter of counsel during the very early days of their mission. If they are not able to handle the additional temptations on their own, encourage them to contact the mission president immediately. Almost all missionaries entering the field honestly believes that they have taken care of all past transgressions. Almost all missionaries who professed to have "taken care of" their sins also came in to see me again sometime during their mission. It isn't that they haven't been forgiven, it seems to be that Satan is successful at getting them to doubt the efficacy of their repentance. Sometimes it was just because they had not learned to avoid similar situations and needed some further counseling.

There is one more area where caution is needed. Most people realize the mission president has the option of shortening or lengthening the missionaries' time of service by up to thirty days to accommodate the needs of the mission. Some parents unwisely see that option as a means of getting their missionary home a month early. Although there are legitimate reasons for shortening a missionary's mission (school starting early, a mandatory date for reporting for military service), these reasons are few and far between. What a powerfully wrong note on which to send a missionary home when the reason is a family reunion, a wedding, or just plain homesickness of the parents. To deprive a missionary of the last month of an experience described by the Lord as "bringing salvation to their soul" (see D&C 4:2, 4) is almost criminal. Even though this may sound like harsh advice, remember that the Lord said: "For many times you have desired of me to know that which would be of the *most worth unto you.* And now, behold, I say unto you, that the thing which will be of the *most worth unto you* will be to declare repentance unto this people, that you may bring souls unto me, that you may rest with them in the kingdom of my Father" (D&C 16:4, 6; emphasis added). Even though our earthly vision may be limited, our faith in the perfect knowledge of the Savior should help us realize that nothing should take precedence over our missionaries' responsibility to serve. Parents are not trying to maliciously sabotage their children's missions—they just haven't thought it through. You will enjoy your missionary's unrestrained association for the rest of your lives. But your missionary will never again have the opportunity to serve the Lord as a single young man and woman.

It almost became a joke to see what excuses missionaries and parents will use to request an early release. Through our experience, the blessing of serving the entire time of the call became abundantly evident. If you are considering asking the mission president to release your missionary early, counsel with your bishop and stake president. Then take your request seriously before the Lord and see what he thinks. You will probably come to the same conclusion we did with our daughters—they are the Lord's children, born through us and now engaged in "their Father's business." Surely we can suppress our will to the will of the Father just as the Savior did when he said: "Father, Thy will, not mine be done."

Happy indeed is the missionary who, in years to come, can look back without regret and say: "I served faithfully and honorably from the day I was called by the Lord until the day he released me." Parents can make that declaration a reality much easier if they stay on the Lord's side.

HELPING YOUR MISSIONARY RETURN WITH HONOR

17

UNDERSTAND ME

ASK ALMOST ANY RETURNED MISSIONARY and they will tell you the same thing: "It is more challenging to adjust to coming home than it was to adjust to the mission field." When you consider the differences between the two situations, you can readily understand. In going to the mission field, everything was preplanned for them— when they would arrive, who would meet and orient them, where they would live and serve, who they would serve with, and a monthly budget to purchase food and necessities. Their daily schedule was mapped out in exact detail— what they were to study, when they were to study as a companionship, what time to leave the apartment, how long they were to stay at members' homes, how long they could stay for dinner appointments, what they should teach during discussions, and rules (not a few) they were expected to follow as outlined in the white handbook. They even knew when their required service would come to an end, the exit process with interviews, who would arrange for the plane flight home, who would get them to the airport, how their luggage was to be cared for, and almost every detail necessary for their safety and success.

Note the contrast when they get off the plane at

home. Yes, their family is usually there to greet them so they have a ride to their home. Occasionally parents arrange for their release interview with the stake president. Very often the bishop has set aside a time for them to report their mission to the ward. Then what? The rest is up to them.

Becoming accustomed to being without a companion can be traumatic. Many report waking up in a panic because their companions are not there. Immediate worry about being disciplined by the mission president for not keeping track of their companion is not easily dismissed until they realize they are no longer on a mission. No one sets the definite daily schedule as they did in the mission. Some returning missionaries try to keep the same study schedule but it just doesn't work. Breaking back into the dating scene can be difficult. How do you act? What can you talk about on the date? As you pick up your first date, do you break the firmly established habit of beginning every meeting with prayer? How do you fit back into your social group without betraying your newly established standards? What should you do for the rest of your life? How do you find a wife or a husband? Will you be able to earn a living? Will the Spirit withdraw because you are no longer a missionary? How do you keep from becoming inactive like some others you have seen return? What if you can't live up to the expectations the family and others have of you? What if the bishop doesn't give you a job in the Church? The questions multiply ad infinitum.

You as parents may not realize why your returned missionary has mood swings. Consider what is going on that you can't see and you may develop more empathy. Does every returned missionary go through the readjustment period? Yes, but not all to the same degree. Some seem to take everything in stride, while others really struggle. Does it mean your son or daughter is failing because he or she is struggling? Not at all. Some of the most dedicated missionaries have the most difficulty accepting the change.

How can you help as parents? There isn't a single simple answer to such a complex question. In the chapter dealing with homesickness, suggestions were given to help you support your missionary in adjusting to the field. Many of those suggestions apply to this "reverse homesickness stage." In reality, one of the most difficult mental times of their young lives is forced upon them. The mission they have been preparing for, dreaming about, serving, and loving has now come to an end. As with the passing of a loved one, the ending of the mission often brings fairly severe mourning. Many of their investigator friends, member friends, and missionary friends are gone without realistic hopes of frequent reunions during mortality. When they have sacrificed their lives to bring others into the gospel, they are rightfully anxious about their staying active in the Church. It is nearly impossible to fly to Africa, Europe, Japan, or Australia frequently to reinforce converts who may be wavering. Just understanding what they are experiencing can help you give comfort and encouragement.

There isn't a given time when missionaries "get over" those lost feelings. Just stay by them until they develop a life outside the mission. If the adjustment period carries on too long, you may want to seek the help of a priesthood leader, a former missionary who successfully readjusted, or even a professional counselor. To pine away longing for the mission field is not healthy. To miss the mission is normal. Returned missionaries are closing the door on a very important chapter in their book of life. In this chapter many have gained a powerful testimony for the first time. They have tasted the sweetness of Christlike service more than ever before. They have learned to love as the Savior loves, more deeply than they imagined possible. They have grown spiritually toward their eternal goals more than they thought possible. Perhaps just discussing the adjustment period with them may be helpful.

One of the very real feelings many returned missionaries report is feeling as if everything they do in life is a step down from what they have been doing. There is a good reason for that, and it is simply—they are right! The Lord told the early brethren in the Church "that the thing which would be of most worth to you will be to cry repentance to the people, that you may bring souls unto me, that you may rest with them in the kingdom of my Father" (D&C 16:6). A young person going through such serious soul searching may feel the only way one can "cry repentance to the people" is to be on a mission. Wrong. The rest of his or her life life will be spent "crying repentance" in one form or another. It just takes awhile to see that the only thing that has changed is the location and frequency of the cry of repentance.

It would be so helpful if wise parents could forewarn returning missionaries about feelings they might experience as they reenter the workforce or the student population. To come home after the first day on the job or the first week of classes and say to themselves: "This is ridiculous! There is no real purpose to this job or these classes. I would rather be back on the mission" is as normal as can be. What do you tell them? Tell them to just hang in there, to not become discouraged or depressed. As they achieve the proper balance in their lives, everything becomes more exciting.

During their missions their entire focus was on the "spirituality" quarter of their wheel. The "physical," "intellectual," and "social" quarters of their wheel were almost totally neglected. Of course when viewed from an eternal perspective, unless they were really unusual, the first nineteen to twenty-one years of their lives were spent focused on the other three-fourths of their wheel at the neglect of the spiritual. So now, instead of the "spiritual" being way out of focus, it has just caught up with the other three. It is not even desirable to have an exclusive focus on the spiritual. Remind them the Savior (our perfect example) "increased in wisdom [intellectually] and stature [physically], and in favour with God [spiritually] and man [socially]" (see Luke 2:52).

You may become somewhat frustrated when your returned missionary decides to stay home and study the Scriptures rather than going to the Young Adult dance. Direct encouragement is sometimes viewed as "meddling" and met with cool resistance. Working through others may be a more productive path. Priesthood leaders, Young Adult leaders, and peers often have more success than we as parents in getting them involved.

Your missionary may suffer from the opposite of the last paragraph. He or she may want to "catch up" all at once by going to every party, activity, and outing the Church and society provides. Again your cautioning warnings may not be welcomed. Funny how a fireside, a sacrament meeting talk, a general conference talk sometimes hits right at the heart better than anything you, as parents, can say. Understanding you still have a supervisory role over your returned missionary but that he or she must be responsible for the choices helps keep the burden of decision-making exactly where it belongs—on your son's or daughter's shoulders.

Not having sufficient money to do very much when they first get home often poses a real challenge for returned missionaries. They may have changed clothing sizes while in the mission field. Their old clothes may be worn out or just out of style. They worry about being able to buy a car so their impact on the family car will be minimized. Getting a job is generally one of the top priorities. It is also very easy for them to lose the proper perspective about work. Some returned missionaries get two or three jobs so they can earn money for school, cars, and social and Church life. Sometimes wisdom is thrown to the wind and needs to be blown back past them to avoid serious consequences. For example, when one job ends at 7:30 p.m,. it is nearly impossible to start the next job clear across town at 8:00 p.m. Even though travel time may not be the problem, unwinding time, eating time, resting time all need to be factored in. When three full eight-hour jobs are taken, it is pretty evident to an adult that something has to give sooner or later. Health is destroyed, accidents from falling asleep at the wheel change lives, failure to grow in other vital areas is neglected when reason is not exercised.

The most productive thing may be to sit down with your returned missionary with a paper, pencil, and calculator and help your son or daughter figure out what his or her goals are and how much it will cost to achieve those goals. The same counsel may be true for those planning to marry. Too few starry eyed couples sit down to see if they can afford to marry. Be careful not to scare them off entirely. If you reflect back, your parents probably didn't think you were ready to marry either! Outline at least the basic necessities and see if their game plan will accommodate the needs and provide at least a little for the unexpected emergencies. Wouldn't life be wonderful if everything always worked the way we planned? Well, it doesn't, as you know, so help your young people be realistic about their future.

It may be necessary to cosign for their car. Teaching them the difference between "needs" and "wants" can be somewhat challenging since their world suggests everything is a need and must be had right now. Usually an honorably returned missionary will be more concerned about putting undue burdens on the family budget than on getting lots of things for themselves. In fact, if you are not cautious, he or she may go without some necessities rather than impact you. There isn't a "right" or "wrong" as to whether you should help or how much you should help. That will vary from one missionary and family to another. However, it is necessary to avoid giving the mistaken impression the world owes them a living. Heaven knows we have too many people in the world who believe it is the burden of society to provide them a comfortable living with all the fringe benefits merely because they exist.

Tuition is expensive. Marriage is expensive. Health insurance is expensive. Cars are expensive. Life is expensive. But when taken a little at a time, life is manageable and fun. When one tries to experience the entire spectrum of life all at once, frustration and disappointment often result. Returning from a mission is difficult if one tries to readjust in all areas all at once. If taken a little at a time, it can be fun and exciting. If lived one day at a time, mortality can be challenging and exhilarating. If we try to live our whole life all at once, we will suffer unnecessarily, with failure as the probable outcome. We can help our children readjust more easily by remembering the Lord's counsel: "Be still and know that I am God" (D&C 101:16). Even during his mortal ministry, the Savior counseled the people to take life one day at a time. He said, "Sufficient unto the day is the evil thereof" (Matthew 6:34).

From the perspective of returned missionaries (and somewhat from our own), life in the future can seem rather foreboding. It is beneficial to teach them that problems "came to pass"—they did not "come to stay." Finances may be a little tight for the first few years they are married. Some of the great bonding experiences of life come while "trying to make ends meet." Sharing experiences that you endured during the early years of marriage can help. Having a favorite uncle or aunt reminisce with them over the "tough times" is also a good way of helping them gain confidence in their ability to cope.

One of the most prevalent attitudinal problems of young returned missionary males is that they feel incapable of successfully meeting the needs of a wife and children. For a long time I thought they were unwilling to accept the responsibility. As I have met with them in countless interviews over the years, it has become evident that they really want to get married but are scared concerning their ability to be equal to the challenge. Too many young people lack an understanding of what it means to "live by faith." They want a rock-solid assurance from Heaven that everything will work out. "How do I know we will still love each other in five years from now?" is not an uncommon question. It is almost as though they think some unseen force dictates whether they are happy or not. We can do a great deal to lessen their feelings of inadequacy if we help them realize they are not the first ones to have such feelings. And to the surprise of many mothers-in-law—they actually have been fairly successful!

It is easy to stand back and criticize that which we do not understand. It is much more difficult, but much more rewarding, to pay the price to understand what is happening in their lives and, using the gospel as the standard, to become part of the solution rather than part of the problem. The reward for you as parents will come as they kneel across the altar in the temple and successfully begin their own little kingdom. Your reward will continue to be multiplied forever as they stand and call your name blessed for being there in a vital support role in the time of their greatest need. Somehow I believe Heavenly Father will also express his appreciation to us for standing in his stead to guide his children back into his presence during these difficult days.

18

....

STAND INDEPENDENTLY VALIANT

FOR THE FIRST NINETEEN OR TWENTY-ONE YEARS of their lives, you nurtured, directed, provided and assumed responsibility for your children. Now they have served honorable missions where they were expected to stand independent and make their own decisions. Without your constant presence, they were put into situations where they could obtain the necessary counsel and aid only from a much Higher Source. Their experiences were probably as varied as their individual circumstances, but the results are the same—they have come to rely on God.

Because of their extended absence, you have not been privileged (except through letters) to witness their rapid maturation. You read what they wrote and intellectually acknowledged the change, but often you may still view them through eyes that vividly recall wiping their nose and changing their diapers. It is difficult to let go. For many parents their sense of worth has been derived, in part, from the essential role they have played in their children's lives. To see their children weaned away physically, intellectually, emotionally, and spiritually can be a traumatic experience.

Almost without being conscious of what is happening, some parents reimpose their controlling influence over their returned missionary son or daughter. Decisions which should rightly be reserved for the young man or woman are dictated by parents who glory (on one hand) at the children's growth but subtly suppress their agency on the other hand. What clothes to wear, where they can and cannot spend money, who they can associate with, activities they can participate in, jobs they can take, directions they can take in school, decisions about dating and marriage all find place on the list of reported incidents of parental interference.

I do not want to suggest that parents should not be involved in the previously mentioned areas and a thousand like situations. On the contrary, your wisdom and counsel provide an invaluable resource to the returned missionary. The problem comes when the direction or control is forced upon them rather than given as counsel. If your son or daughter has learned the valuable lessons of life which normally present themselves in the mission field, he or she will willingly seek counsel, collect as much information as possible, and carefully weigh the "pro's" and "con's" of every major decision. But the freedom to make the decision should be jealously guarded. If we stop to think about our child's situation, it is not so different from our own. Would you like someone dictating whether you could buy a car or not and which one you can purchase? Would you feel irritated if someone put restrictions on your hard-earned paycheck, dictating how you could spend it? Would you prefer that someone tell you, to the smallest detail, how to discipline your children although they do not know your children as well as you do nor do they have to live with the consequences of that discipline?

Therein lies the real key: They, not you, must live with the consequences of their decisions. It seems only reasonable, therefore, that they should have the final say in the decision. If things go wrong, who can they blame if they were the ones who chose? If things go well, shouldn't they have the satisfaction of knowing they made wise choices? It is not an easy decision on your part to know where to draw the line on your involvement.

You are still the presiding authorities in your home. You have established certain rules calculated to help the home run smoothly. Whoever, whether related or not, comes to your home should be expected to abide by the rules. Even a returned missionary son or daughter should have the rules explained to them and what is expected laid out in some detail. Then they have a choice: If the rules seem too restrictive, they are free to move out and get their own apartment or they can voluntarily abide by the rules. One of their options should not be to stay at home and make their own set of rules.

One of the difficult lessons the world seems to be fighting is clearly taught by the Lord. He said: "There is a law, irrevocably decreed in heaven before the foundation of this world, upon which all blessings are predicated—And when we obtain any blessing from God, it is by obedience to that law upon which it is predicated" (D&C 130:20–21). There seems to be an implied corollary which says: "There are consequences to every action. If you pick up the one end of a stick, the other end will always and inescapably follow. Actions have consequences." For example, one of the rules in our home is that no member of the family has the right to verbally or physically abuse any other member. Since we have normal children, there are plenty of opportunities to reinforce the rule. If a son or daughter absolutely refused to abide by the rule to the hurt of another member, and we had done everything in our power over a long a period of time to help that child conform, he or she would be faced with an ultimatum: Cease and desist or find another place of residence. Children should not have the option of destroying the home as they indulge in their unacceptable behavior. Thankfully, to this point, we have been sufficiently successful in explaining the rules, and the gospel principles behind those rules, that our children have not tested the promised consequences. Nevertheless we have all witnessed families that have been destroyed because cancerous behavior of one or more members was not excised in a timely enough manner.

If your children have served honorable missions, confrontations of the previously described nature will likely never happen. However, they are adults and they do want to make decisions. Where those decisions do not affect the smooth running of the family, allow them to choose. Our experience, both in our own family and with missionaries who have reported back, suggests when freedom is provided for decision-making, children willingly seek counsel before making major decisions. It is difficult sometimes to restrain ourselves from making decisions for them.

Obviously, the most far-reaching and long-lasting decision young people will make is who to marry. When you take the time, in family home evening, or family counsels, or just in the times you sit around and discuss life, to help them see the principles behind successful marriages, they will generally make wise choices. If you are disturbed about a particular person they are dating, attack the concern—not the person. Because marriage includes the new person in your family, you do have a right to counsel. Nevertheless, the ultimate decision belongs to the young person. If there is a serious difference of opinion, you may profit by asking yourself some serious questions: "If my son or daughter chooses to marry this person in spite of my protest, what will my reaction be?" "Is my dislike of my son's or daughter's potential mate sufficiently strong to warrant my severing all ties with my child?" "Is my dislike of this person going to cause 'cold war' feelings every time he or she comes to visit?" "Is my disapproval worth forfeiting any possible relationship with my future grandchildren from their marriage?" Many other like questions need to be seriously considered.

Sometimes our dislike of the potential mate is based on principles that we need to correct. Discrimination based on social status, economic standing, or conditions of his or her family over which he or she has no control can cause unnecessary stress. Eventually we expect to enjoy life together in the celestial kingdom. It may be advantageous to remember the Lord's stern warning: "That you may be equal in bonds of heavenly things, yea, and earthly things also, for the obtaining of heavenly things. For if ye are not equal in earthly things ye cannot be equal in obtaining heavenly things. For if you will that I give unto you a place in the celestial world, you must prepare yourselves by doing the things which I have commanded you and required of you" (D&C 78:5–7). Unfortunately, I do not have sufficient space to discuss the law of consecration, but we can stand back and, using eternal perspective, put priorities on our prejudices. I can't think of very many things which would cause me to disinherit my children and cut off all future association.

We may have had dreams for our children on what we wanted them to become in life—doctors, lawyers, engineers, educators, musicians, business owners. More importantly, we would do well to ask what they want to be in life.

We are seeing a new trend in the United States. Well-established, very successful professionals are reevaluating their job satisfaction and making midlife changes. Business executives are buying small farms and ranches because they have always wanted to work with animals and the land. One computer analyst quit his job to start a fly tying business in northern Idaho. The list is endless. If our generation would be perfectly honest, many would admit they secretly admire those who are brave enough to do what they really want to do rather than be pigeonholed in a job or career they dislike.

We may look at this rising generation as "irresponsible" because they are more focused on personal fulfillment than on the acquisition of temporal wealth. I am far from suggesting that we encourage another "flower-power" generation like that in the early '60s. But whether a person is a mechanic or a college professor is not as important as how well they enjoy their jobs and how honest they are in that profession. Perhaps we would all do well to remember counsel given by President David O. Mackay on the sequence of priorities on which the Savior will require an accountability from us:

Let me assure you, Brethren, that someday you will have a personal Priesthood interview with the Savior, Himself. If you are interested, I will tell you the order in which He will ask you to account for your earthly responsibilities.

First, He will request an accountability report about your relationship with your wife. Have you actively been engaged in making her happy and ensuring that her needs have been met as in individual?

Second, He will want an accountability report about each of your children individually. He will not attempt to have this for simply a family stewardship but will request information about your relationship to each and every child.

Third, He will want to know what you personally have done with the talents you were given in the pre-existence.

Fourth, He will want a summary of your activity in your Church assignments. He will not be necessarily interested in what assignments you have had, for in his eyes the home teacher and a mission president are probably equals, but He will request a summary of how you have been of service to your fellowmen in your Church assignments.

Fifth, He will have no interest in how you earned your living, but if you were honest in all your dealings.

Sixth, He will ask for an accountability on what you have done to contribute in a positive manner to your community, state, country and the world." (From notes of Fred A. Baker, managing director, LDS Church Department of Physical Facilities, June 1965)

It is always difficult for me to be humble enough to be taught by those younger than myself. However, with the events associated with the second coming of the Lord unfolding as rapidly as they are, perhaps we would be wise to learn a few lessons from our valiant sons and daughters. If the effect of your counsel and "help" is negative, stand back and see if you are encroaching on the sacred turf of "agency." Interestingly, the term *free agency* is never used in the Scriptures. There is definitely a price associated with the right to choose. We were willing to fight in the pre-earth life for the right to choose, is it any wonder we resist when people and governments try to rob us of God-given rights here on earth?

If we could learn to be rightly proud when we teach our children to stand independent of us, we would be developing into a person who more closely resembles our Heavenly Father. Note how many times he comes down and makes decisions for you. If you ask, he is willing to guide and counsel, but NEVER to decide for you. Can we, in our quest to become like God, afford to do any more?

19

Using the Lessons

ALTHOUGH THERE IS NORMALLY A LETDOWN when a missionary returns home, it does not need to be a testimony-shattering experience. More than a couple of missionaries report the feeling of emptiness which follows their release by the stake president. Some go through periods of depression when they feel life is over. Schooling is not as relevant as missionary work. As we continue to stand as a support system for them, it would be easy to turn on the Church and complain that they don't do more for these vulnerable young people. However, by this time in their lives, it is more expedient that they do something for themselves. No one paved the way and smoothed out all the rough spots during their mission. No one is hired to make life easy for them now they are home.

If we stand back from the immediacy of the present and try to take a broader view, we can see opportunities for continued service in furthering the work of the latter days. What have they been doing that has been so rewarding? The most obvious answer is "teaching the gospel." Unless you live in an entirely different situation than most, there are still multiple opportunities to continue teaching.

One of the most frequently voiced complaints against returned missionaries is they come across as feeling superior to those who have not gone or those who returned home from missions some time before. If they really learned their lessons in the mission field, they will realize the greatest among us was designated as the servant of all. The Savior said: "But whosoever will be great among you, shall be your minister: And whosoever of you will be the chaffiest, shall be servant of all" (Mark 10:43-44). If you detect an arrogance creeping in, remind them of Mark 10:42-45, Matthew 23:11, and Luke 22:24-30. The Savior leaves little room for those who are "big in their own eyes." Generally, returned missionaries are humble, fun people to be around because of the depth of their experience and the extent of their knowledge. If they start to glory in their own importance and understanding, they can become obnoxious in a hurry, at home or in the classroom.

We have found one of the keys to continued humility is continued growth. Too many missionaries who have been faithful in their studies during their missions decide to take a breather. There isn't anything more stale than a returned missionary who is trying to give the greatest zone conference talk they ever heard fifteen years after returning home. As they study the doctrine, help them focus more intently on the basics. Too many want to get off into areas where the Lord in his wisdom has chosen to say very little. We tried to encourage our missionaries to follow the pattern of the Lord and his leaders. If they have said very little about a subject, we would be wise and safe to follow suit.

Almost on the flip side of the "know-it-all" coin are those returned missionaries who clam up and refuse to share what they know and what they have experienced. One of the powerful growth agents in the mission field was the requirement to give continually of themselves. Because life is complex and problems not easily solved, it required their constant pleading with Heavenly Father to give them understanding. Those of us who are older recognize that marriage, child-rearing, and Church positions afford continuing opportunities which require our constant pleading for Divine guidance.

Occasionally a tired returning missionary will say: "I've given two years to the Lord, now I'm going to take a couple of years for myself." What a counterproductive attitude. The very factor which made them great is what they are choosing to eliminate from their lives. A wise parent will continue to foster activities calculated to keep the young person serving. It is very often easier for us to do a task ourselves rather than try to chase our children down and prevail on them to do it. It may be easier but it is not more productive. Create areas where your returned missionary can serve and feel needed and useful.

Some returned missionaries, feeling the exhilaration of freedom, go "ward hopping." They go for endless weeks attending welcome home meetings of their friends. They hold no positions in the Church because they are never in one ward long enough to receive a call. But if they cease serving, they start dying spiritually. It is sometimes painful for parents to sit them down and commit them to continued service in their local ward or singles' ward.

Missionaries are almost forced, by the work they do, to keep God continually in their thoughts. Once they return home it is easy to let day after day go by without seriously thinking about God, the meaning of life, life after death, doctrine, service, the prophet and other leaders—the very elements which make earth life tolerable and directed. Wise King Benjamin, during his farewell address to his beloved people, seemed to worry about their losing sight of their eternal goals. He queried: "For how knoweth a man the master whom he has not served, and who is a stranger unto him, and is far from the thoughts and intents of his heart?" (Messiah 5:13). If you really want a superlative spiritual experience, study the Scriptures daily with your returned missionary. His or her insights will not only edify and thrill you but will serve as a catalyst to keep him or her growing and focused on eternal things.

The great prophet/Lawgiver, Moses, seemed to have the same concern about the people forgetting. In his farewell letter to a people he had literally sacrificed his life for, he said:

> Hear therefore, O Israel, and observe to do it; that it may be well with thee, and that ye may increase mightily, as the Lord God of thy fathers hath promised thee, in the land that floweth with milk and honey.... And these words [scriptures], which I command thee this day, shall be in thine heart: And thou shalt teach them diligently unto thy children, and shalt talk of them when thou sittest in thine house, and when thou walkest by the way, and when thou liest down, and when thou risest up. And thou shalt bind them for a sign upon thine hand, and they shall be as frontlets between thine eyes. And thou shalt write them upon the posts of thy house, and on thy gates. . . . Then beware lest thou forget the Lord! (Deuteronomy 6:3, 6-9, 12)

People do not fall away from the Church overnight. It is a slow process which happens day by day as they withdraw themselves from the light of the gospel. In a day when apostasy was prophesied to be rampant, we can continually guard ourselves and our children against personal apostasy by bringing them into an environment of pure light. The Scriptures can create that environment. Having dealt with many misoriented people over the course of a lifetime who have been infected with the spirit of apostasy, I have seen they are the last to know the light has gone out. In fact they will (and usually do) argue endlessly, claiming they are right, while the Church has gone astray. The Prophet Joseph Smith gave us this caution and key:

> O ye Twelve! and all Saints! profit by this important Key—that in all your trials, troubles, and temptations, afflictions, bonds, imprisonments and death, see to it that you do not betray heaven; that you do not betray Jesus Christ; that you do not betray the brethren; that you do not betray the revelations of God, whether in the Bible, Book of Mormon, or Doctrine and Covenants, or any other that ever was or ever will be given and revealed unto man in this world or that which is to come. Yea, in all your kicking and flounderings, see to it that you do not this thing, lest innocent blood be found upon your skirts, and you go down to hell. All other sins are not to be compared to sinning against the Holy Ghost, and proving a traitor to the brethren.

> I will give you one of the Keys of the mysteries of the Kingdom. It is an eternal principle, that has existed

with God from all eternity: That man who rises up to condemn others, finding fault with the Church, saying that they are out of the way, while he himself is righteous, then know assuredly, that that man is in the high road to apostasy; and if he does not repent, will apostatize, as God lives." (*Teachings of the Prophet Joseph Smith*, pp. 156-57)

It is difficult to have had the responsibility to evaluate attitudes and performance for the past eighteen months or two years and now to have someone say: "Don't criticize." Nevertheless, that is what must be done. There is so much positive work to do as we help "perfect the saints" that there is hardly time to dwell on areas of needed improvement outside our own stewardship.

No matter where you go in the world you can identify "Mormon missionaries." They are distinguished not only by their behavior but also by their looks. Too many young people seem to believe they must stand out in a crowd to be outstanding. President Spencer W. Kimball made the following statement:

I want you to know it is hard for me to be disappointed, and I rejoice in the blessings of the Lord daily. But a few things disappoint me occasionally and one of them is the returned missionary who, after two years of taking great pride in how he looks and what he represents, returns to this campus or some other place to see how quickly he can let his hair grow, how fully he can develop a moustache and long sideburns and push to the very margins of appropriate grooming, how clumpy his shoes [can] get, how tattered his clothes, how close to being grubby he can get without being refused admittance to the school. That, my young returned missionary brethren, is one of the great disappointments in my life. . . .

Please, you returned missionaries and all young men who can understand my concern in this matter, please do not abandon in appearance or principle or habit the great experiences of the mission field when you were like Alma and the sons of Mosiah, as the very angels of God to the people you met and taught and baptized. We do not expect you to wear a tie, white shirt, and a dark blue suit every day now that you are back in school. But surely it is not too much to ask that your good grooming be maintained, that your personal habits reflect cleanliness and dignity and pride in the principles of the gospel you taught. We ask you for the good of the kingdom and all those who have done and yet do take pride in you. (*Teachings of Spencer W. Kimball* [Salt Lake City: Bookcraft, 1982], pp. 592–93)

In spite of this prophetic warning, too many otherwise honorably returned missionaries try to push the limits of propriety in their dress and grooming. Aping the world scarcely describes a focused Latter-day Saint who is determined to pay whatever price is required to earn a spot in the celestial kingdom. As parents, sit down with your missionaries before the mantle wears completely off and discuss dress and grooming. If they realize the magnitude of their call, they will also know they can never really "return" to the old ways. That neutral ground they stood on before their mission no

171

longer exists. They will forever be classified as a "returned missionary." What a high honor! What an awesome responsibility! Their baptismal covenant will be much more pertinent to them now than before their mission. You will recall Alma giving the following explanation of our responsibilities as members: "Yea, and are willing to mourn with those that mourn; yea, and comfort those that stand in need of comfort, and *to stand as witnesses of God at all times and in all things, and in all places that ye may be in*, even until death" (Mosiah 18:9; emphasis added).

These righteous returned missionaries must be made to understand they will forever bear their testimony for one side or the other. Either they will bring honor and attention to the Savior and his Church by their dress and grooming as well as by their behavior, or they will aid the cause of the adversary because of their desire to "be like all the nations" (1 Samuel 8:20).

One of their greatest assets as far as employment, dating, church opportunities, and social activities is the way they look. As parents we can help reinforce their clean-cut look by keeping their eyes on the Brethren and our local leaders. "Look, dress, and act like they do and you'll always be safe."

As your missionary reports his or her mission in sacrament meeting, you will see a more polished, confident young man or woman than ever before. A mission just does that to them. They will be more powerful in presenting their ideas, more logical in their ability to reason, and more persuasive in the personality of their presentation. Does that have to end with their welcome home speech? Certainly not. With encouragement from you, they can continue to polish those communication skills. They should have lost the fear of talking with adults, leaders, the wealthy, the poor, the homeless, the businessman or the executive. Armed with those skills, your missionaries should be a desirable addition to any workforce. Help them realize the value on their resumé the mission provides. They need not be ashamed of putting their "salesmanship" experience, their "leadership" experience, their "supervisory" experience, or their "reliability" report in a letter reciting their assets. Where else in the world can young people get such "on-the- job-training" in so broad a field as they can in missionary work. Unfortunately, many feel hesitant mentioning their mission when they apply for jobs or service positions. If they have served in a foreign mission where a language is required, they may be able to qualify for unique positions where translating or being bilingual is a prerequisite. Many of our California missionaries returned to become translators for government officials for the refugee communities. Who better qualified than a young person who knows the language, the people, the customs, the culture, and who loves them?

This chapter could easily become an entire book in itself. There are so many lessons of life missionaries learn while on a mission which can enrich their own and everyone else's lives if they will continue to share. Your maturity as a parent may be the catalyst to get them thinking about how they can effectively continue using their newly acquired skills and knowledge.

20

CONTINUING THE TEST

THERE HAS BEEN AN UNDERLYING CURRENT throughout this book. It has been that challenges have been encountered throughout the growing-up years and continued during missionary service. Life was not intended to be easy, obstacles have been encountered, setbacks have been experienced, and disappointments have had to be overcome. Many times we do not understand the reasons behind the trials, but seldom are we given the choice as to whether we go through the test or opt for some easier trial.

For some reason, after having endured the buffetings of Satan for the first twenty-one to twenty-three years of life, many returning missionaries seem to think the test is over. Life will be sweet and easy from here on. No more trials, no more disappointments, no more setbacks, nothing but smooth sailing. What a shock to the system when they discover that the tests only become more complex and more challenging. If they are successful at maintaining their spirituality, they need to expect continued trials in ever-increasing frequency and intensity.

Brigham Young taught an important lesson about why we are required to endure trials:

I ask, is there a reason for men and women being exposed more constantly and more powerfully, to the power of the enemy, by having visions than by not having them? There is and it is simply this—God never bestows upon His people, or upon an individual, superior blessings without a severe trial to prove them, to prove that individual, or that people, to see whether they will keep their covenants with Him, and keep in remembrance what He has shown them. Then the greater the vision, the greater the display of the power of the enemy. And when such individuals are off their guard they are left to themselves, as Jesus was. For this express purpose the Father withdrew His spirit from His Son, at the time he was to be crucified. Jesus had been with his Father, talked with Him, dwelt in His bosom, and knew all about heaven, about making the earth, about the transgressions of man, and what would redeem the people, and that he was the character who was to redeem the sons of earth, and the earth itself from all sin that had come upon it. The light, knowledge, power, and glory with which he was clothed were far above or exceeded that of all others who had been upon the earth after the fall, consequently at the very moment, at the hour when the crisis came for him to offer up his life, the Father withdrew Himself, withdrew His Spirit, and cast a veil over him. That is what made him sweat blood. If he had had the power of God upon him, he would not have sweat blood; but all was withdrawn from him, and a veil was cast over him, and he then pled with the Father not to forsake him. "No," says the Father, "you must have your trials, as well as others."

So when individuals are blessed with visions, revelations, and great manifestations, look out, then the devil is nigh you, and you will be tempted in proportion to the vision, revelation, or manifestation you have received. Hence thousands, when they are off their guard, give way to the severe temptations which come upon them, and behold they are gone. (*Journal of Discourses* 3:205-6)

What a powerful insight! Crystallizing what he taught, then we should expect an equal and opposite temptation for every spiritual experience, revelation, or insight we receive. These are not trials we should search out—they will find us. From our study of the Scriptures, it seems apparent the test may precede or follow the spiritual experience. Joseph Smith had not even enjoyed the "pillar of light" before the adversary made every possible attempt to destroy him. His famous but very humble recital of those events leaves little doubt in the reader's mind of the severity of the test. He records:

... I was seized upon by some power which entirely overcame me, and had such an astonishing influence over me as to bind my tongue so that I could not speak. Thick darkness gathered around me, and it seemed to me for a time as if I were doomed to sudden destruction ... not to an imaginary ruin, but to the power of some actual being from the unseen world, who had such marvelous power as I had never before felt in any being. (Joseph Smith—History 1:15-16)

In other accounts the trial follows the spiritual experience. In Moses chapter 1 is recorded an experience in which Moses is permitted to stand in the presence of God and see the entire world and all of the inhabitants thereof. As the presence of the Lord withdraws from Moses, he experiences a "power failure" to the extent he falls to the ground. It requires "many hours" before he regains his normal strength. Almost immediately Moses revives, Satan appears in visual form and challenges Moses to worship him, claiming himself as a son of God. A bitter struggle ensues between Moses and Satan in which Moses, apparently relying upon his own power, tries to banish Satan. Satan becomes increasingly annoyed at Moses' steadfastness and drawing upon his demonic power he rants and raves, the earth quakes and trembles, but finally, succumbing to the power of the Only Begotten, Satan departs. Interestingly, another vision bursts upon Moses and carries him to an even higher level of spirituality and understanding (see Moses 1:1–34).

Using these two great prophets as examples of what Brigham Young taught, it seems necessary that we warn our children to keep their guard up. To the Regional Representatives and General Authorities of the Church on several occasions, President Gordon B. Hinckley taught that the greatest tragedy in the Church is the losing of new members, members, and returned missionaries to inactivity. One wonders if this great tragedy could not be greatly diminished, if not eliminated, if we could alert the unwary Saints to Satan's tactics?

At times we set up incorrect standards or expectations about how things ought to be. When early death deprives us of a loved one, if we are not careful, we are tempted to turn on God or wonder if we have fallen into Divine disapproval. In the mission field, the young people were taught to put these apparent tragedies into eternal perspective. For some reason, when they return home, many forget to continue applying that same standard.

In order to help them see how ludicrous it is to instruct God on how to manage his affairs, I refer to a childhood example. My mother would invite a number of her friends to our house for an afternoon of socializing and refreshments. Not wanting to be interrupted by little children, she would instruct us to either play in the other room or go outside. Being intensely interested in what they were doing, we generally played in the adjacent room. Each room had a keyhole lock where a skeleton key could be used to lock the door. When the key was removed, a person could see a small portion of the adjacent room by looking through the keyhole. We would take turns peering through the keyhole to see what Mom and her friends were doing. At one time she would be looking off to the left laughing at something within her view, but hidden from us because of the limited size of the keyhole. Another time she would be looking to the right, seriously listening to someone in that part of the room hidden to us, but clearly within her view.

So it is with our Heavenly Father. He has an unobstructed view of our premortal past and a perfect view of our postmortal future. Everything to God is "one eternal now." Joseph Smith taught: "The great Jehovah contemplated the whole of the events connected with the earth, pertaining to the plan of salvation, before it rolled into existence, or ever 'the morning stars sang together' for joy; the past, the present, and the future were and are, with Him, one eternal 'now'" (*Teachings of the Prophet Joseph Smith*, pp. 220).

When we exercise faith in Heavenly Father, we find those things which seemed so unfair to us now, when viewed from an eternal perspective, are Divinely just. When job offers don't work out, engagements are broken, health is lost, accidents happen or mental and emotional problems are experienced, we need to be wise enough to help our children keep their faith strong. For those who would like some additional insight, you may want to read President Spencer W. Kimball's pamphlet "Tragedy or Destiny." The same article is found in his book *Faith Precedes the Miracle* [Salt Lake City: Deseret Book, 1972], pp. 95–106.

As a teenager I spent my junior year of high school with a friend whose parents were teaching at the Church high school in American Samoa. There was a single road running the length of the island. Based on our tortuous experiences riding the bus to Pago (the capital city), we were convinced the road had been constructed by the devil and taken from its original location in the dark underworld. It seemed to be a series of connected potholes, punctuated frequently by protruding boulders. When there was a smooth segment (which wasn't often!) the road would jog, twist, and turn from any position other than a straight course. Even being young and healthy, after riding to town it felt as if our kidneys had taken a severe beating. Loud and frequent were our complaints about the road.

One day during the Christmas vacation, my friend and I climbed the Mapusaga Rainmaker, an almost vertical 1,500 foot mountain adjacent to the road. I received there one of the great revelations of my young life. From atop the mountain we could see from one end of the island to the other. All of those purposeless bends had meaning—a jog here to avoid a bog, a turn there to miss a village, another curve to avoid a boulder, cliff or unseen obstacle. From our new vantage point everything seemed to have purpose. To my utter amazement, all the potholes so painfully experienced while on the road had disappeared from view from where we stood.

I believe our experience on the mountain has helped me keep a better perspective on life. The Lord is stating a true principle when he revealed: "Therefore, he giveth this promise unto you, with an immutable covenant that they shall be fulfilled; and all things wherewith you have been afflicted shall work together for your good, and to my name's glory, saith the Lord" (D&C 98:3). When I hear of returned missionaries becoming disillusioned because of the difficulty of the way and subsequently falling into forbidden paths, I wonder where are the parents and adult leaders to help them "stand on top of the mountain" where, with unobstructed view, we can see forever?

The trials of the latter days promise to provide high adventure to those who dare meet the challenges head on. What an eternal shame to have proven valiant in the premortal existence, received assignments and foreordinations there, proven faithful during the difficult growing up years, having received the priesthood and the temple endowment, served an honorable mission, only to return home, let down our guard, and be swept away by the vicious lies and devious tactics of the adversary.

Will life always be so challenging? Probably. But as our spiritual muscles harden to the task, it does not seem like such an impossibility. I would hate to see our young people look with despair towards the future. This is the greatest of all times to be alive. Most certainly we will face challenges unparalleled in the history of the earth. But if the Lord did not feel we were up to the challenge, he certainly would not have placed us in the situation.

Too many returned missionaries who are looking at the woeful state of the world and noting its rapid decline decide to forego marriage and raising a family. Only wise parents and leaders can help them see the tremendous blessings they are forfeiting by such an unwise choice. Some of our young people are making equally unwise decisions concerning the necessity of advanced schooling, claiming the world will not be intact when they have graduated. Those strains are not new. They have been heard by countless generations as Satan tries to lull us into inactivity in any and all productive areas. Sharing the wisdom you have accumulated over a lifetime may be the factor that causes them to reconsider their unwise decisions.

Someday life will radically change for the world. Until that time, it would do well for us to remember the invitation to "carry on" given by the Savior as he recounted the events leading to his glorious Second Coming. He said: "Blessed is that servant, whom his lord when he cometh shall find so doing" (Matthew 24:46; see also Luke 12:43, and Joseph Smith Translation, Matthew 1:50). By helping our young people keep their eyes trained on our leaders, we can insure the ever-increasing challenges we are required to meet will not overwhelm us. How blessed you are to be entrusted with the vital role of keeping their faith alive until the fire of testimony burns too brightly to be extinguished by Satan's chilling efforts.

21

WHEN A NOBLE ONE FALTERS

LIFE DURING THE DAYS PRECEDING the great second coming of Christ has been prophesied for millennia as being of unparalleled difficulty. Prophets during our day have echoed the warnings of their ancient counterparts. President Joseph Fielding Smith said:

> Our Savior promised that the days preceding his second coming will be typical of the days of the flood. A glance at the 6th chapter of Genesis will reveal the conditions of the world in the days of Noah and the flood and the reason for the cleansing by water. This comparison is not to be taken figuratively, but literally, as it is given. The world today is corrupt and filled with violence as it was at that earlier day, for now, as then, all flesh has corrupted its way upon the earth. The Lord promised that he would never again destroy the entire world with a flood of water, but he did promise to cleanse it the second time with sword and with fire. (Joseph Fielding Smith, *Doctrines of Salvation* [Salt Lake City: Bookcraft, 1954], 3:20)

One could be tempted to become discouraged with the "gloom and doom" of latter-day conditions. Certainly the objective of this book is not to portray a negative outlook on life. There is so much good and so many unparalleled opportunities for those who are holding firmly to the "iron rod." Unfortunately, a few return from honorable service and wander off into forbidden paths and are temporarily lost. In spite of the best efforts of parents, priesthood leaders, and Church members, the lure of the world overcomes reason and good judgment in a few good souls.

It would be wonderful if a simple solution could be found. Past experience suggests some will learn only in the "school of hard knocks." Although we hate to see them suffer, they still have their agency. Without my trying to give an exhaustive evaluation of the Savior's parable of the "Prodigal Son" found in Luke 15:11–32, we may profit from a couple of insights. It is interesting to note when the younger son came to the father and demanded his "portion of goods that falleth to me," his father complied with his request. In modern terms, the father actually provided the financial means for the riotous living of his son! He contributed to the delinquency of a minor!

The parable is well known, so a recital of all the points is not necessary. However, for those whose children have chosen a divergent path, it would be profitable to reread the entire parable from beginning to end. You will weary yourself looking for the verse where the father assumes responsibility for his son's deviant behavior. If your children insist on learning the lessons of life the hard way, you may be consoled to know eventually they will learn. Ask yourself a simple question: "If I had known how to be a better parent, would I have done it?" My firm belief for most faithful

Latter-day Saint parents is a resounding "Yes!" Even now, as I look back at those early years of marriage and note some of the dumb mistakes I made, I wonder why I did not do things better. When rationality returns I realize I did not know how to do any better when I was that age. Rather than punishing yourself for something you should have done, it seems more productive to continue studying, learning, and practicing, so you will not make the same mistakes again. You may also have multiple opportunities to help others who are following after you avoid the same mistakes.

There is another small phrase in the parable often overlooked by grieving parents. It reads: *"And when he came to himself."* It was not when his parents decided he had gone far enough. It wasn't even when the bishop or priesthood leader called him up short. It was not until he sat in the deplorable circumstance his choices had projected him into that he realized there must be a better way. Sometimes it is a revelation of the first magnitude for people to realize their severe headache is due to their continually hitting their own head on the floor. What seems so obvious to us, may not be interrelated in their mind.

Over the years we have all watched the devastation alcohol abuse brings to a family. Too many realize too late how false and artificial the glamour of infidelity really is. Destruction of self-esteem, breakup of the family, loss of confidence of the children for parents, disease, death, destruction of society, all combine to bear solemn testimony that Satan really is a "liar from the beginning" (D&C 93:25). Innocent drugs thought to be and promoted as "harmless" just a generation ago have been identified as permanently life threatening and irreversibly mind altering. Yet foolish people continue their carefree quest for happiness in violating the commandments of God.

Probably the first virtue we need to exercise in dealing with wayward children is "patience." We are under Divine commission to warn them of the consequences of their behavior. The ancient prophet Ezekiel puts into proper perspective the responsibility we should have towards our children in warning them of their deviant ways. He records:

> When I say unto the wicked, O wicked man, thou shalt surely die; if thou dost not speak to warn the wicked from his way, that wicked man shall die in his iniquity; but his blood will I require at thine hand. Nevertheless, if thou warn the wicked of his way to turn from it; if he do not turn from his way, he shall die in his iniquity; but thou hast delivered thy soul. . . . Say unto them, As I live, saith the Lord God, I have no pleasure in the death of the wicked; but that the wicked turn from his way and live: turn ye, turn ye from your evil ways; for why will ye die, O house of Israel? . . . The righteousness of the righteous shall not deliver him in the day of his transgression: as for the wickedness of the wicked, he shall not fall thereby in the day that he turneth from his wickedness; neither shall the righteous be able to live for his righteousness in the day that he sinneth. When I shall say to the righteous, that he shall surely live; if he trust to his own righteousness, and commit iniquity, all his righteousness shall not be remembered; but for his iniquity that he hath committed, he shall die for it. (Ezekiel 33:8-9, 11-13)

Former righteousness will not be sufficient to save us in the day of our wickedness. Some young people say, "I have given two years to the Lord, now it is time for me to take a couple years for myself!" What a poor choice. Should death overtake us in our hour of transgression, at best we depart this mortal probationary state with a huge question mark over our head. Ezekiel also holds out hope that once repented of, our former transgressions will not stand to condemn us before the judgment bar of God.

As the prophet Ezekiel pointedly noted, if we fail to warn the wicked man of his wicked ways, he will die, but his blood will be required at our hands. There seems to be a certain accountability associated with having the truth. If we bear fervent testimony, whether the testimony is accepted or rejected, we transfer the responsibility from our shoulders to the person to whom we have born only testimony. If they choose to accept our testimony and conform their lifestyle to the truth, we will greatly rejoice together. If, however, the testimony is rejected, there will be no excuse, and payment for the transgression will shift to the shoulders of the transgressor.

How far do we need to go in warning our children? Again, it would be nice to have a definitive answer. However, we do have the prophetic example of righteous father Lehi in dealing with his two rebellious sons, Laman and Lemuel. At the end of Lehi's remarkable dream about the tree of life as recorded in 1 Nephi 8, Nephi records:

And it came to pass after my father had spoken all the words of his dream or vision, which were many, he said unto us, because of these things which he saw in the vision, he exceedingly feared for Laman and Lemuel; yea, he feared lest they should be cast off from the presence of the Lord. And he did *exhort* them then with all the feeling of a tender parent, that they would hearken to his words, that perhaps the Lord would be merciful to them, and not cast them off; yea, my father did *preach* unto them. And after he had preached unto them, and also *prophesied* unto them of many things, he *bade* them to keep the commandments of the Lord; and *he did cease speaking unto them.* (1 Nephi 8:36–38; emphasis added)

It appears father Lehi did everything he knew how to do, and then there came a logical point where he was only making matters worse by continuing his efforts. If Mormon had been able to write more than a "hundredth part" (see Words of Mormon 1:5), perhaps we could have seen how he arrived at the point of knowing he had done everything possible. Perhaps the Spirit bore an unmistakable witness to his soul that the Lord had accepted his teachings as sufficient.

When our pain and anguish become so great, it is easy to lose the proper eternal perspective. Try "zooming out" to get the big picture. Standing from a vantage point removed from the present, we can recall a premortal past of indeterminate length (probably many thousands, if not millions of years) in which your son or daughter had proven faithful and true. Using the Lord's reference for computing time, we remember that one day with the Lord is comparable to 1,000 years with man (see Abraham 3:4). Using some simple mathematics, every year with us is equivalent to 1 minute and 26 seconds with God. Considering you have a twenty-five-year old son, he would have been out of the presence of God for a grand total of 35 minutes and 50 seconds! If he has been struggling with keeping the commandments for the past three years, he has been "less active" for 4 minutes and 18 seconds! After an eternity of faithfulness, can we really afford to "write them off" after less than 5 minutes of wavering?

The Prophet Joseph Smith gave some very comforting insights to our present discussion. "So long as a man will not give heed to the commandments, he must abide without salvation. If a man has knowledge, he can be saved; although, if he has been guilty of great sins, he will be punished for them. But when he consents to obey the Gospel, *whether here or in the world of spirits*, he is saved" (*Teachings of the Prophet Joseph Smith*, p. 357; emphasis added). It is not for us to judge whether a person has sinned away his exaltation. The Lord wisely counseled: "Leave judgment alone with me, for it is mine" (D&C 82:23). In no way should this reasoning be construed to condone sin or an undisciplined lifestyle. I only wish to leave judgment where it rightfully belongs. From our many experiences, we can all attest that hearts do soften over time, lives change, conversion takes place—sometimes late in life—and covenants neglected for decades can be made. Ordinances are performed both for the living and for the dead.

A second statement by the Prophet Joseph Smith continues the above thought. At the funeral service of his good friend Elder King Follett, he said:

You mourners have occasion to rejoice, speaking of the death of Elder King Follett; for your husband and father is gone to wait until the resurrection of the dead—until the perfection of the remainder; for at the resurrection your friend will rise in perfect felicity and go to celestial glory, while many must wait myriads of years before they can receive the like blessings." (*Teachings of the Prophet Joseph Smith,* p. 359; emphasis added)

The inference is that after myriads of years they may be able to receive "like blessings," which were described as "celestial glory."

When one considers the Savior's description of the suffering of those who have not taken advantage of his atoning sacrifice, only a fool would opt to balance the scales of justice in that manner. He said:

Therefore I command you to repent—repent, lest I smite you by the rod of my mouth, and by my wrath, and by my anger, and your sufferings be sore—how sore you know not, how exquisite you know not, yea, how hard to bear you know not. For behold, I, God, have suffered these things for all, that they might not suffer if they would repent; *But if they would not repent they must suffer even as I*; Which suffering caused myself, even God, the greatest of all, to tremble because of pain, and to bleed at every pore, and to suffer both body and spirit—and would that I might not drink the bitter cup and shrink. (D&C 19:15-18; emphasis added)

Life is so designed by the Divine Hand to insure the great eternal lessons will be learned. We do not need to feel obligated to be the executioner of eternal justice. The "punishment that is affixed" (2 Nephi 2:10) cannot be avoided except on conditions of repentance. Errant children also cannot hope for the "happiness which is affixed" (ibid), when they transgress the law. Samuel the Lamanite drove this point home when he stood atop the walls of the city of Zarahemla and declared the sealed fate of the rebellious Nephites:

> But behold, your days of probation are past; ye have procrastinated the day of your salvation until it is everlastingly too late, and your destruction is made sure; yea, for ye have sought all the days of your lives for that which ye could not obtain; and ye have sought for happiness in doing iniquity, which thing is contrary to the nature of that righteousness which is in our great and Eternal Head. (Helaman 13:38)

Without the burden of being either the executioner or the excuser, we are free to enjoy life, doing everything the Lord inspires us to do for the salvation of our children. If we constantly petition for Divine guidance and are willing to do whatsoever the Lord inspires us, we may yet be the instrument the Lord uses to bring back these precious souls. Giving up, condemning, cutting off, embarrassing, ridiculing, or ostracizing them seldom accomplishes Divine ends because they are satanic means. ". . . persuasion, by long-suffering, by gentleness and meekness, and by love unfeigned, by kindness and pure knowledge . . . , without hypocrisy, and without guile" (D&C 121:41–42) can work miracles because we are using God's means to accomplish his ends.

If the Lord has not given up on our children, can we afford to do less? Elder Richard G. Scott gave the following comforting advice in the April 1988 general conference:

I will suggest seven ways you can help. First—Love without limitations. . . . Second—Do not condone the transgressions, but extend every hope and support to the transgressor. . . . Third—Teach truth. . . . Fourth—Honestly forgive as often as is required. . . . Fifth—Pray trustingly. . . . Sixth—Keep perspective. When you have done all that you can reasonably do, rest the burden in the hands of the Lord. . . . One last suggestion—Never give up on a loved one, never! (*Ensign*, May 1988, pp. 60-61)

Remembering they are His children and that they have been born only physically through us helps keep our challenges in a more correct perspective. Someday we will see Divine purpose for all of these tests and be perfectly content that "He doeth not anything save it be for the benefit of the world; for he loveth the world, even that he layeth down his own life that he may draw *all* men unto him" (2 Nephi 26:24; emphasis added). Remember, the game is not over until the final buzzer sounds! Many games are won by valiant, last-minute efforts. Carry on!

22

"WELL DONE THOU GOOD AND FAITHFUL SERVANT"

THE BEST HANDBOOKS IN THE WORLD for raising righteous, valiant children are the Scriptures and the teachings of the Latter-day prophets. For almost 6,000 years, a kind, wise Heavenly Father has tutored his children through those learning experiences calculated to help them pass the tests of mortality en route to immortal glory. When you would be born, how far you would travel, how long you would live in mortality were all known before the foundations of the world were ever laid.

The great prophet Moses declared: "When the most High divided to the nations their inheritance, when he separated the sons of Adam, he set the bounds of the people according to the number of the children of Israel" (Deuteronomy 32:8). Confirming the same thought and enlarging upon it, the Apostle Paul said: "And hath made of one blood all nations of men for to dwell on all the face of the earth, and hath determined the times before appointed, and the bounds of their habitation" (Acts 17:26). In our day the Lord revealed through the Prophet Joseph Smith: "For there is a time appointed for every man, according as his works shall be" (D&C 121:25).

Think of it! Saved for this very hour according to the foreknowledge of God to perform a work only you are capable of doing. Children destined to take their rightful positions among the "noble and great ones" (see Abraham 3:22) have been entrusted to your watch care. While vast armies of unseen demons do everything in their power to stop the work of God, they are destined to fail. The Prophet Joseph Smith made this stirring declaration:

No unhallowed hand can stop the work from progressing: persecutions may rage, mobs may combine, armies may assemble, calumny may defame, but the truth of God will go forth boldly, nobly, and independent, till it has penetrated every continent, visited every clime, swept every country, and sounded in every ear, till the purposes of God shall be accomplished, and the great Jehovah shall say: The work is done." (Dean Jessee, *Papers of Joseph Smith "Church History."* 1842 [Salt Lake City: Deseret Book, 1989], p. 436)

Perhaps we need to remind ourselves often that hidden (sometimes deeply hidden!) beneath those rough exteriors are men and women who received their foreordination as missionaries way back before the world was created. Joseph taught: "Every man who has a calling to minister to the inhabitants of the world was ordained to that very purpose in the Grand Council of heaven before this world was" (*Teachings of the Prophet Joseph Smith*, p. 365). They have a destiny to fulfill and they will fulfill it. Most of us are willing to admit the superior potential of the preparing generation. We are less prone to admit the magnitude of those who have been entrusted to give them their first lessons here in mortality—you!

Joseph Smith again puts well our responsibilities if we would be successful with our children. He taught: "Thy mind, O man! if thou wilt lead a soul unto salvation, must stretch as high as the utmost heavens, and search into and contemplate the darkest abyss, and the broad expanse of eternity—thou must commune with God" (ibid., p. 137). While it is definitely true that there has never been more expected of any generation than there is of this one, it is equally true there has never been more expected of those preparing them for the battle than there is of us. The alarming trends of child abuse, juvenile delinquency, gangs, teen pregnancy, teen suicide, drug abuse, and wanton destruction of life and property by the young all suggest a generation of parents who have grown tired of the battle. As regrettable as these trends are, it would be wonderful if Church members were spared—however, we are not.

This is not a day of standing back and throwing stones. No one is criticizing the efforts currently being made. But we cannot rest yet. As we listen to and heed the teachings of our leaders, we will find Satan's power decreasing in our own and our children's lives. As we seek answers in the holy temples, we will enjoy seasons of revelations compensating for our deficiencies. As we continue to discuss in priesthood, Relief Society, and Sunday School classes the challenges we are facing, sharing with each other ideas that work, we will find the task of directing tomorrow's leaders is not as foreboding as the adversary would have us believe.

When we have gone as far as we can possibly go, we can ask for and expect to receive Divine assistance when human wisdom fails. To see the great numbers of faithful young men and women entering the MTC is consoling. As Satan loudly proclaims the impossibility of the task, faithful parents just keep on succeeding. The Savior described a tender scene to be acted out in all its glory when he comes again. It is well known but even more apropos when applied to preparing missionaries. In Matthew 25:34–40 the Savior described a partial judgment to be conducted at the Second Coming. He states:

> Then shall the King say unto them on his right hand, Come, ye blessed of my Father, inherit the kingdom prepared for you from the foundation of the world: For I was an hungered, and ye gave me meat: I was thirsty, and ye gave me drink: I was a stranger and ye took me in: Naked, and ye clothed me: I was sick, and ye visited me: I was in prison, and ye came unto me. Then shall the righteous answer him, saying, Lord, when saw we thee an hungered, and fed thee? or thirsty, and gave thee drink? When saw we thee a stranger, and took thee in? or naked, and clothed thee? Or when saw we thee sick, or in prison, and came unto thee? And the King shall answer and say unto them, Verily I say unto you, Inasmuch as ye have done it unto one of the least of these my brethren, ye have done it unto me.

It seems ironic the righteous seemed to be unaware of the service they were rendering. They almost sound surprised as though the Savior had made a mistake in selecting them as the chosen ones. They seem to be in a state of mild denial because they were not the flashy, stand-up-front-and-take-charge ones. Consider briefly what they had done:

I was an hungered and ye gave me meat. What greater hunger can we satisfy than our children's hunger to know the word of God from the Scriptures and the Latter-day leaders?

I was thirsty and ye gave me drink. As they thirst for understanding and insight, who more appropriate to guide them to the "well of Living Water" than a parent who diligently teaches the gospel during family home evenings and as "teaching moments" occur?

I was a stranger and ye took me in. How often during their growing up years has a cold, cruel world turned its back on them? Who opened their homes, hearts, and refrigerators without condition? When attitudes were in the obnoxious, disagreeable stages of development, who still loved them unconditionally?

Naked and ye clothed me. Literally, yes, but who also taught them to "put on the whole armor of God?" Who prepared them for the buffeting of the world by securely wrapping the cloak of acceptance and love around them in spite of the ridicule their peers thoughtlessly heaped on them?

I was sick and ye visited me. Think of those endless days and long nights you literally sat at their bedside tending to their feverish needs. But more significantly, think of the times when they were sick with sin or failure or rejection and you provided the anchor they needed for their soul. "Ye visited me" suggests that you were willing to go to them rather than always waiting for them to come to you. Sometimes parents have to enter environments laden with worldly sickness to retrieve their wavering children.

I was in prison and ye came unto me. At times that scene has been literally reenacted. More significantly, many young become imprisoned to habits, substances, or language which retard their progress as literally as steel bars restrain their physical movements. Caring support, never-giving-up attitudes, and being forever "there" for them can and do win precious souls back from the awful grasp of the adversary. Even "friends" in sin abandon them when punishment looms on the immediate horizon. You have gone to them in their hour of need when they erroneously concluded all hope was gone.

The Savior will bring his reward with him. Those who have struggled through the heat of the battle will receive their crowns. In the words of Joseph Smith: "Brethren, shall we not go on in so great a cause? Go forward and not backward. Courage, brethren; and on, on to the victory!" (D&C 128:22).

I can think of no more difficult assignment than parenting during these difficult days. Is it possible to *Prepare with Honor* those malleable souls entrusted to our watch care? Can a modern day "Army of Helaman" withstand the onslaught of satanic temptations and present themselves worthy and prepared for the foreordained task ahead of them? With your help they can! Noting the opposition the adversary throws at the Lord's missionaries every minute of every single day, is it possible to help these valiant young people *Serve with Honor* the Lord who called them to the work? It is and the Lord knows you are the ones who can help them accomplish this all but impossible task. There are so many potential stumbling blocks to fall over, and so many potholes to fall into, that without your help these noble servants must look back with some regret at less than honorable service. Noting the challenges we face now, and will continue to face as we enter the battles yet future, is it really possible to help our young people

Return Home with Honor from their missions and live lives worthy of acceptance by the Lord. It is, indeed and you are the ones honored by the Lord to give the "behind the scenes" encouragement and direction necessary to help them avoid making progress-retarding mistakes.

What a joyous season is yet ahead when we can sit around eternal campfires and reminisce about the battles we have fought and won. I wonder if brothers and sisters from billions of other worlds will be very interested in our experiences. To be entrusted with the awesome responsibility of preparing the world for the Second Coming is unparalleled, on this or any other world. That we should take a few bumps and bruises is no surprise. That we will succeed is assured. In the words of the Savior, who knows all things: "Well done, thou good and faithful servant: thou hast been faithful over a few things, I will make thee ruler over many things: enter thou into the joy of the lord" (Matthew 25:21).

So many promised blessings await you as you prepare the next generation of missionaries. Perhaps the Lord was using his counsel to Thomas B. Marsh as a medium for helping parents who are challenged in the raising of children. He said: "Behold, you have had many afflictions because of your family; nevertheless, I will bless you and your family, yea, your little ones; and the day cometh that they shall believe and know the truth and be one with you in the church. Therefore, thrust in your sickle with all your soul, and your sins are forgiven you, and you shall be laden with sheaves upon your back, for the laborer is worthy of his hire. Wherefore, your family shall live" (D&C 31:2, 5).

Someday (it may not be until the next life) your children will come to you and thank you for your valiant efforts in their behalf. When you see them crowned with crowns of glory on their heads as they receive their exaltation, your joy will be full and your reward complete. Then you will know for sure that all your efforts have been worth the pain.

Fired with that eternal vision, we must redouble our efforts to *Send Forth with Honor* those who have been lovingly entrusted to our watch care. God help us not to falter during these final minutes before the great second coming of the Lord.

Index

Acceptance; see *Peer Pressure*

Adjustment; to civilian life, 148-156

Adversary; 13, 20, 24, 51, 61, 73, 81, 85, 86, 92, 113, 125, 175, 180, 194, 197

Age; when planning a mission, 10

Answers; finding, 29, 30, 194

Anxiety; producing activities, 24, 28, 92

Apostasy; 169

Assignment; 97, 129

Attitude; irresponsible, 71; positive, 51, 66-67, 86-87, 132; self-centered, 48, 64-65, 167

Baptisms for dead; family experience, 14; opportunity for salvation, 15

Behavior; assume responsibility for, 71, 83, 191, see *Responsibility*

Benson, Ezra Taft; chosen youth, 77-78; endowments, 19; low self-esteem, 76; obligation to serve, 7; sacred privilege, 7

Bible; 18, 33, 49, 74, 79, 80-82, 87, 95, 152, 155, 166, 168, 172, 181, 183, 185, 192, 195, 198

Blaming others; 72

Blessings; 22, 120, 175, 198; from covenants, 2, 23

Book of Mormon; 18, 30, 42-43, 57, 59, 61, 63, 65, 66-67, 81, 82, 87, 92-93, 95, 168, 172, 175-176, 186-187, 189-190, 191, 193

Books; basic, 30

Budgeting; 46, 148, 174

Buffetings; 69, 84, 87, 91

Calling; 97, 109, 113

Celestial Kingdom; 73, 85, 171; visual reminder of, 16

Cleanliness; 45, 47, 171; teaching, 68-71

Challenges; 4, 5, 51, 116, 117

Character traits; deficiencies, 64-65, 194; of missionaries, 51, 54, 114

Chaste living; 60

Choice; to serve, 4

Chosen-Youth; 12, 77-80

Clothes; 32, 33, 45, 91, 170

Commitment; 11

Communication; getting along with others, 48, 53

Companions; 47, 64, 69, 71, 91, 100, 103, 104, 106, 115, 130, 131, 134, 149

Confidence; 76; from scripture memorization, 52-53

Conflicts; 42, 48, 53, 114, 131-132

Contact; parents to missionary, 5, 101-106, 133, see also *Disobedience* and *Procedures*

Correspondence; to mission president, 96-97, 100-103, 105-107, 113-115, 125, 132, 133; overcome discouragement, 91-94, 96, 115, 119-121, 139, 141

Covenants; prevent divorce, 23; see also *Temple*

Creativity; 51

INDEX

Criticism; 73, 74, 125, 170, 194

Databases; scripture study, 29
Decision; to serve, 6, 11
Decision-making; 125, 153, 158, 160,
    161, 164; taught by parents, 54-57
Depression; 41, 150, 152, 165
Difficulty; with mission experience,
    2, 50, 51, 93, 94, 97-98
Diligence; 107-108, 140, 141
Discipline; learn lessons by, 37-39;
    with love, 35-36
Discouragement; see
    Correspondence
Dishes; washing, 70
Disobedience; to mission rules, 101,
    105-107, 109, 184-185, 190;
    telephone calling cards, 101-103
Disqualify; to serve mission, 48, 59
Doctrine and Covenants (D & C); 6,
    17, 20, 22, 23, 35, 36, 38, 41, 60,
    61, 74, 82-86, 95, 99, 107, 120,
    122-123, 128, 139, 144, 145, 151,
    155, 159, 161, 180, 184, 188, 189,
    190, 192, 197, 198

Early return; embarrassment, 45, 96,
    132, 145; how to avoid, 3, 92, 97
Education; 7, 140
Emergencies; 102-104
Emotions; 92, 93, 116, 118, 149, 151;
    stability, 41-43, teen years, 34, 35
Endowments; 16, 19, 20
Enlargements; see *Talks*
Ensign; 8, 10, 27, 78, 191
Examples; by parents, 58; use of
    pictures, 13, 25
Excellence; 52
Excuses; 71-73, 101, 145, 186
Experiences; social 58, 62-63

Failure; 39, 97, 132, 196
Faith; 11, 94, 155, 179, 181
Faltering; 180, 183-184, 199
Family; 11, 13, 27, 28-29, 140
Family Home Evening; use in
    preparation for mission, 14, 27,
    64, 65
Family Resource Book; 28

Farewells; motivational value, 9
Feedback; 69-70, 115
Finances; 46, 106; upon return,
    153-155
Flashbacks; 44, 143
Focus; 118, 124, 125, 134, 141, 152, 177
Food; 45-46, 91
Forgiveness; 144
Friends; 62, 64, 149
Friend; 10

Garments; temple, 91
Gifts; 107, 135
Goals; 92; school and occupational,
    7, 153, 162, 173, 181
God; Nature of, 164; relying on, 157
Going home; 97, 139
Goliaths; emotional and physical,
    40-49
Gospel; 5, 16, 25, 27, 29, 30, 93
Gossip; 73
Gratitude; 107
Greeny; new missionaries, 107
Grooming; personal, 32-33,
    170-171; teaching good habits,
    33, 171
Growth; spiritual, 23, 126, 131, 166,
    196
Guilt trips; 71-72

Haircuts; reminders, 33
Holidays; 96, 138
Holy Ghost; see *Spirit*
Homesickness; 89-98, 135, 137, 140
Home with Honor; 4
Honesty; 45

Investigators; 53, 105, 122, 139, 150

Jesus Christ; 82, 87, 93, 112, 140,
    141, 155, 166, 175
Journal; 99-100
Judging others; 73, 92, 111, 125;
    potential mates, 161

Keys; assume responsibility, 71, 159;
    develop desire to go to Temple,
    17; to give service, 49, 92
Kimball, Spencer; 6-7, 170-171, 179

Leadership; 111-117
Lessons; by example, 58, 68, 105, 183
Letter; from First Presidency-March 4, 1993, 40, 48, 49 see *Mission;* qualifications
Letters; 9, 10, 91, 99, 100, 105; types to avoid, 112, 113, 119-122, 131, 133
Letting go; parents, 157
Listening; to children, 54

Marriage; 16, 19, 23, 109, 126, 153-154, 160-161; priority for women, 8, 109
Maturity; spiritual, 9, 157
Meals; 45-46, 135
Mediocrity; 52, 76, 108
Men; length of mission, 95; fears about future; 155
Mission; 45, 48-51, 74, 81; alternatives to, 47; qualifications, 40, 48, 49; stages, 137, 138, 141
Mission President; 8, 31-33, 44, 55, 62, 64, 67, 72, 74, 75, 84, 96-97, 100-103, 105-108, 111, 114, 115, 122, 127-129, 132, 135-136
Missionary Handbook; 72, 99, 100, 105, 148
Mourning; end of mission, 149-150

Negativism; 76, 133; how to avoid, 67, 85-86, 140
New Era; 10, 25, 79
Nonmembers; 15, 21

Obedience; 68, 87, 99-111, 159; to leaders, 45, 72
Obstacles; parents prepare children for, 13, 42, 174, 197
Opposition; learning to handle, 12
Ordinances; 15, 188
Overextending; socially and financially, 153

Passing the buck; 57, 58
Parents; 74, 76, 120, 121, 145, 151, 156, 167, 173, 194-197; lives as an example, 16; movitators, 51, 69, 70
Past; 45, 143
Patience; 50, 55, 131, 185

Peer pressure; 59, 60, 62, 64, 66
Perfection; 86, 124
Perspective; 92, 93-95, 124, 178, 180, 187
Persevere; 142
Physical effort; required for mission, 11, 45, 50, 74, 93, 119, 121, 138
Practice; 58
Praise; 53, 69, 72, 73
Prayer; 8, 10, 90, 91, 108, 115, 122, 130, 191
Pre-ordained; 78-84, 192-193
Preparation Day; (P Day) 100, 105, 112, 140, 141
Preparation; parents helping missionary, 2, 8, 11, 50
Prepare with Honor; 3
Priesthood; 14, 25, 80, 110
Primary; 14, 120
Principles; godliness, 17, 35-39
Problem-solving; teaches patients, 50, 55, 131
Procedures; contacting missionary, 102-103, 105, transfers, 132-134
Promises; 95-96, 120, 128
Prophets; 78-87, 110, 162-163, 177; also see alphabetical listings
Protection; 20

Rationalization; 65, 71, 73, 101
Reading; 95
Reinforcement; positive, 8
Rejection; coping with, 41, 74
Relationships; 148
Repentance; suffering in spite of, 43, 189; lack of/effect on mission, 45-45
Responsibility; 44-46, 109; accepting full, 57-58, 71-73, 160, 183, 186
Revelation; rights to, 23, 194
Role Models; 9, 61
Rules; obeying, 49, 91, 102, 107, 115, 124-125, 159, 160

Satan; 11, 12, 23, 41, 44, 51, 60, 69, 77, 84, 143-144, 174, 177, 181, 184, 194, 195

INDEX

Scripture study; family, 30, 58, 95;
memorization, 52-53; 91
Self-control; 31, 34, 68, 83, 126
Self-esteem; 29, 76-77, 159
Self-pity; 113, 131, 139
Sensitivity; to others' feelings,
64-65, 106-107, 122
Serve with Honor; 3
Service; 76, 92, 137-145, 151, 163,
165, 167
Sin; consequences, 51, 61, 196
Skills; leadership, 111, 173; social,
62, 6465
Smith, Joseph; 21-22, 31, 83-84,
85-86, 169-170, 176, 178,
188-189, 193, 194
Smith; Joseph Fielding, 21, 81,
108-109, 182
Speeches of the Year; 56
Spirit; evidence of, 17, 18, 21-23,
38, 99; withdrawal of, 73,
101-102, 107, 128, 175, 187
Spiritual; housecleaning, 45;
experiences; 93-94, 168, 175
Sports; analogies, 28, 77, 118-119,
138, 191
Support; lack of, 9; need for, 11,
117, 119, 136, 156
Suffering; consequences of
behavior, 43-44, 93
Swearing; 35, 58

Talks; preparing, 25; main ideas, 25;
format, 26, 29
Tapes; 107
Tasks; break down, 69
Teaching; 24; Gospel by participation,
16, 25; home and visiting, 26, 165
Teenagers; responses to parents,
34, 65-66
Telephone calls; see
*Correspondence with Mission
President* or *Disobedience*
Temper; controlling, 42, 43, 58
Temple; covenants in, 21; family
visits to, 13, 14, 16, 17, 23, 156;
repeated visits for understand-
ing, 18; scriptural symbols in, 18

Temptations; while on mission, 3,
20, 48, 84, 85, 113, 175
Testimony; 26, 104, 172, 181, 186
Tests; from Heavenly Father,
113-114, 174, 191; from Satan, see
Buffetings
Tolerance; of differences, 74
Trainer; 112
Transfers; 129-131 see *Mission*
Trials; 104, 113, 174, 175
Trust; 127

Walls; washing, 45, 47
Willingness; to change, 75
Word of Wisdom; 6, 16, 43, 60
Work; temple and missions, 1, 105
Worthiness; 43
Women; length of mission 95;
marriage, 7-8
Woodruff, Wilford; 80

Young, Brigham; 176-177